ERNST MARTI (1903–1985) was born in Switzerland and studied medicine in Vienna and Basel. He worked as a doctor in Solothorn and Arlesheim, Switzerland, where he met Ita Wegman. She entrusted him with the task of researching the etheric forces, to which he then devoted his whole life. He worked for more than 40 years as a doctor in Basel and founded the Society of Anthroposophical Doctors in Germany. He gave many lectures and courses for doctors as well as the general public and wrote numerous essays and papers that were published in specialist periodicals. He died at the Ita Wegman clinic.

THE ETHERIC

Broadening Science through Anthropsophy

Volume 2: The World of Formative Forces

Ernst Marti

Translated by Paul King

TEMPLE LODGE

Temple Lodge Publishing Ltd.
Hillside House, The Square
Forest Row, RH18 5ES

www.templelodge.com

Published in English by Temple Lodge 2018

Originally published in German in a single volume under the title *Das Äetherische* by Verlag Die Pforte, Basel 1989
Translated from the 3rd edition, Zbinden Verlag 2014

A CIP catalogue record for this book is available from the British Library

ISBN 978 1 912230 13 6

Cover by Morgan Creative
Typeset by DP Photosetting, Neath, West Glamorgan
Printed and bound by 4Edge Ltd., Essex

Contents

1. The Sensory Qualities of the Visible World

	Light	Sound	Life
Warmth	Air	Water	Earth
	Density/ Electricity	Gravity/ Magnetism	Atom/ Nuclear force

The 'Universal Formula' or the Constitution of World and Man
[from Vol. I, page 82]

The universal formula shown in tabular form above is the foundation of our world. But this foundation is invisible. The ten entities are imperceptible. We do not find them as sense perceptions.

The constitutive entities in the table are the world as possibility—the world *en dynamei* according to Aristotle, or the *'potential world'* according to Thomas Aquinas. It has to be brought to manifestation—*en energeia, in actu*—by other forces. What Thomas Aquinas could only formulate conceptually can today be found in reality.

We live in a sensory, perceptible world. When we perceive this world through our senses we find a multitude of qualities and characteristics: colours (red and blue); tones (high and low, loud and soft); smells, tastes, weights, forms, textures of touch, etc. We experience these qualities as sensation.

The question now arises: How do the ten entities of the universal formula become perceptible, sensory qualities?

Let us approach this with a very specific question, e.g. how does colour (say, red) arise in the world?

When we look to modern physics for an answer, it says: colour is an electromagnetic activity which, at a specific frequency, gives us the colour red. Physics openly admits that it cannot explain how these physical vibrations are transformed into the inner sensation of 'red' through the sense organ of the eye.

According to Goethe, colour arises by the interaction of light and darkness. For Goethe light and darkness are spiritual (i.e. super-natural) principles which he detects as effective realities in nature. However, for colour to appear on surfaces, a third element is needed according to Goethe which he called 'dimness' [or 'turbidity'] (*Trübe*).

In the first volume of this book, we found through anthroposophical understanding that etheric forces and central forces, being polarities, do not combine directly in nature but collaborate in a third principle—the elements. Through the co-operation of light-ether and the corresponding darkness/central force (density + electricity), colour does arise, but needs an appropriate carrier, the air-element. The perceptible reality of colour arises only when ether, central force and element all work together.

From this triune unity physics extracts the central-force portion and discovers the electrical conditions. Goethe, not yet recognizing the active forces, found only their spiritual principles as light and darkness, and the elemental portion appeared vaguely for him as the concept of 'dimness'.

Just as physics abstracts the electrical component from the totality of colour and ends up with something imperceptible, so also would this be the case if one were to abstract the ether or the element. Only the interaction of the three sources together generates the phenomenon of colour.

This threefold interaction holds true for all the qualities and phenomena of our world. This reveals one of the primary facts of the sense world, namely, that it is perceptible by virtue of the collaboration of three factors, three world principles—the ethers, the elements and the central forces. It will now be a question of seeing this triune principle of manifestation at work within the full range of our universal formula. For this we must allow the triads that belong together to interact in our thinking. We can depict the threefold connection symbolically in the following diagram.

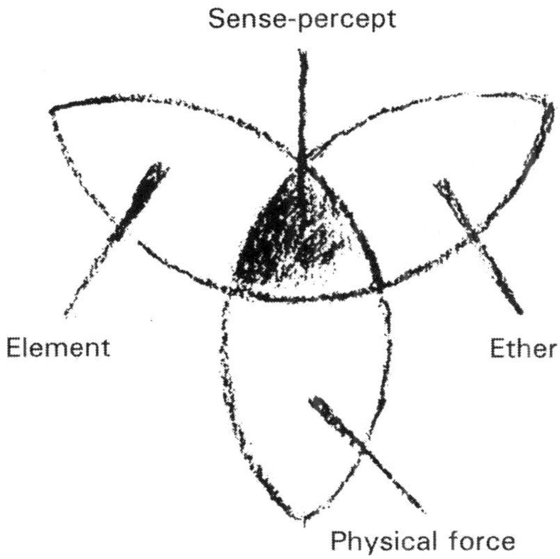

Diagram 1. Collaboration of the three Entities

The triangle created jointly by the three entities represents the sense-percept (the categories of manifestation.)

In reality one of the three principles always predominates; this gives rise to three kinds of phenomena: those in which a) the ether predominates; those in which b) the element predominates; and those in which c) the central force predominates.

When in the air triad

a) the light-ether predominates, degrees of brightness appear, light colours;
b) the air-element predominates, aeriform, gaseous conditions arise, and middle colour tones (e.g. green);
c) the central forces predominate (density + electricity), degrees of darkness appear, dark colours and different densities.

When in the water triad

a) the sound-ether predominates, harmonies arise, sounds, and chemical arrangements;
b) the water-element predominates, liquids arise;
c) gravity predominates, specific weights arise.

When in the earth triad

a) the life-ether predominates, organic forms arise, living bodies;
b) the earth-element predominates, objects arise, inorganic bodies;
c) the atomic force predominates, parts appear, particles.

When in the fire triad

a) the warmth-ether predominates, organic time arises, the phases of biological life;
b) the warmth-element predominates, fire appears;
c) physical warmth predominates, specific temperatures arise.

The manifest world around us is sense-perceptible by virtue of the appearance, in four evolutionary stages, of *time, space, movement* and *form.*

These results can be summarized in a similar way in a table of constituents, and result in a table of the basic secondary qualities (categories of manifestation) of the sense-perceptible world (*Materia secundaria*).

Basic order of secondary qualities

	Time	Space	Movement	Form
a)	Organic time. Bio-chronology	Degrees of brightness. Colours	Sounds. Chemical arrangements	Organic bodies, organisms
b)	Fire	Gases	Liquids	Objects
c)	Specific temperatures	Degrees of darkness. Specific densities	Specific weights	Atoms

The full diversity and multiplicity of our present sensory world arises through the interaction and interplay of the above phenomena. Through combinations of these, other qualities and attributes arise such as smells, tastes, degrees of hardness, tensile strength, etc. Sensory phenomena show still further laws, for example the enlivening of the air and water triads—tone manifests in air, and conversely colour needs water. Likewise, in the realm of central forces, electricity and magnetism combine into electromagnetism. The almost insoluble difficulty of separating mass and matter is connected with this. The interconnections of every fact of physics are to be found here.

Perception of the above categories of manifestation occurs through the sense organs. Physiologists have recognized that the usual five senses—sight, hearing, smell, taste and touch—are insufficient and have postulated others such as sense of life, pain, balance, movement, another person, etc. Rudolf Steiner's research discovered early on that there are twelve senses altogether, completing the usual five as follows:[1]

Sense of:

word	sight	hearing	thought
[another's] 'I' or Ego	smell	taste	touch
warmth	[one's own] movement, [proprioception]	balance	life

Arranged like this they correspond to the above basic order of the categories of manifestation and show how our senses are connected with the phenomena of the sense-perceptible world.

2. The Nature of Sensation and Morphogenic Forces

At this point a critical question could present itself for the reader. Rather than just colours, sounds, and forms etc., do I not rather perceive definite things—the colour red, the musical interval of a third C-E, the form of a rose, a leaf or a flower, the weight of a vase, etc.? Within the range of the sense-perceptible world we find only specific things, each of which can be differentiated, specified and individualized according to its attributes in terms of the categories of manifestation. Is not something else required to bring about this 'specific-ness' of sense-world reality?

This begs a fundamental question: What is it that unites the entities that belong together in a particular manifestation? Put concretely: who or what causes the collaboration of light-ether, electricity and element so that the colour red appears? Is it pure coincidence, or can we find a definite impetus or discernible catalyst?

An answer can be found by looking at the relation of sensory stimuli to sense impression as inner experience. Present-day physics is aware that it does not understand how the sensory stimulus of any sense organ—not even of the eye where it is the most straightforward—becomes inner sensation. We therefore refer here to Rudolf Steiner's *Introduction to Goethe's Scientific Writings* and the chapter on *Archetypal Phenomena*:

> Let us investigate the facts very objectively. Let us assume that a definite sensation arises in our consciousness. It arises in such a way that it simultaneously refers us to some object from which it originates. If I have a sensation of 'red', as a rule I connect it at the same time, by virtue of the content of this awareness, with a particular location, that is, an area in space or the surface of an object to which I

ascribe that which is expressed in this sensation. (An exception to this is when, due to an outer influence, the sense organ responds in its characteristic manner, as when from a blow to the eye I have the sensation of light. We can disregard such instances, in which incidentally the sensations never arise with their usual definition. As exceptions they cannot instruct us about the nature of the subject.)

As soon as I have the sensation of 'red' connected with a definite location, I am referred by it to an object of the outer world as the bearer of this sensation. Now I can ask myself: What spatial-temporal processes take place in this object while it appears to me with the attribute of the colour red? It then becomes evident to me that mechanical, chemical or other processes present themselves in answer to my question. I can proceed further and investigate the processes that took place on the path from the object to my sense organ so as to mediate to me the sensation of red. Here again nothing other than kinetic processes or electrical currents or chemical changes can present themselves as the mediator. I would have the same result if I could investigate the further mediation from the sense organ to the centre in the brain. What is mediated along this entire path is the perception in question of red. *How* this perception appears in any thing [in any section or segment] along the path from the stimulus to the perception, depends entirely on the nature of that thing [segment]. The sensation is present at every stage from the stimulus to the brain, but not as such, not explicitly, but in a way corresponding with the nature of the thing [segment] at each point.

This points to a truth, however, which is capable of shedding light on the entire theoretical foundation of physics and physiology. What do I learn from an investigation of any thing [i.e. any section of the stimulus-perception path] that is involved in a process arising in my consciousness as sensation? I learn no more than how that thing responds to the action proceeding from the sensation, or in other words: how a sensation *expresses* itself in any object of the spatial-temporal world. Far from such a spatial-temporal process being the *cause* that triggers the sensation *in* me, the very opposite is rather the case: the spatial-temporal process is the *effect* of the sensation in a thing extended in space and time. I

> could interpolate as many things as I liked on the path between stimulus and sense organ—in each would occur only what can occur according to its nature. Therefore it is only the *sensation* that is present in all these processes.[2]

Not a usual idea! Sensation is the primary factor that determines colour. To make headway here, sensation itself must be investigated. Rudolf Steiner does so as follows:

> What do I experience inwardly when I designate a sensation as my own? I experience that in my thinking I connect it to my individuality, that I extend my field of knowledge to the sensation; but I am not aware that I create the *content* of the sensation. I am only aware of the connection to myself; the quality of the sensation is a factor determined by itself.[3]

This is a key to understanding the appearance of red in the world. Physics confirms the vibrations but does not ask who sets these very vibrations of red in motion. It does not look for an instigating agent. If, however, I can see the connection of my sensation of 'red' with the rose, then the statement—'the spatial-temporal process is the *effect* of the sensation in a thing extended in space and time'—applies.

But sensation must not now be misconstrued as something merely subjective, for 'the quality of the sensation is a factor determined by itself'.

Red is an objective quality in the world, arising as sensation in my subjective consciousness and in the outer world as the sensory quality of red in a rose. My sensation of red and the red in the rose have a common cause or origin.

This brings us to a problem of great consequence. Forces must exist in the world which can take the imperceptible entities and transform them into perceptible sensory qualities. These quality-creating forces are of a higher order than the entities themselves—the ethers, elements and central forces—for they take hold of these and draw them together, thereby bringing the sense-perceptible world and all its qualities into manifestation. These forces can be called *morphogenic [or formative] forces*.

The following statement by Rudolf Steiner is intelligible only by means of an understanding of morphogenic forces: 'Our sense picture of the world is the sum of the metamorphosing content of our perception without a material basis.'[4]

In the inorganic world morphogenic forces cause the appearance of colour, sound, forms, specific weights, substances, etc. In the organic world they call forth the full phenomena of life appearing in every organism as form, vital functions, and specific substance. Supersensible investigation perceives morphogenic forces, and experiences their existence directly. Our task now will be to find them through their manifestation in the sense world.

Before we do so, however, we must first clarify the origin of morphogenic forces.

3. On the Origin of Morphogenic Forces

What is the origin of these morphogenic forces that causes the invisible world to bring forth perceptible forms, colours, sounds, substances and specific movements of life?

In the first volume of this book we saw that the origin of central forces is the centre-point of the earth. By contrast, the cosmic circumference, the sphere of the heavens, is the peripheral origin of the ethers. These forces are essential for the phenomena of life, as Rudolf Steiner explains in *Grundlegendes für eine Erweiterung der Heilkunst* [Foundations for an extended art of healing)]: All inorganic processes

> show themselves as governed by forces raying out from the essential nature of matter, from—relative—mid-point to the periphery. Organic processes demonstrate matter governed by forces acting from outside inwards, towards the—relative—mid-point. In the transition to life, matter must extricate itself from the out-raying forces and submit to the in-raying ones.
>
> Now, every kind of earthly matter and process has its out-raying forces from the earth and in association with the earth. It is matter, in the form investigated by chemistry, only inasmuch as it is a part of the body of the earth. If it is to come to life, it must cease to be a mere part of the earth. It disassociates itself from the earth. It is integrated into forces that radiate in to the earth from all sides from extra-terrestrial regions. When we see substance or a process unfolding as life, we must picture it as having withdrawn from the forces working from the centre of the earth, and having come into the realm of other forces that have a circumference, not a centre.
>
> These forces work in from all sides, as though striving towards the centre of the earth. *They would have to completely dissolve, tear apart, all form in earthly matter if the influences of the heavenly bodies beyond the earth did not enter and mingle in this arena of forces and modify the dis-*

> *solution.* We can see what this involves by considering the plant. In plants, the substances of the earth are lifted out of the realm of earthly influences. *They strive towards formlessness. This transition into formlessness is modified by influences from the sun and such like from cosmic spaces.*[5]

This quote draws attention to 'heavenly bodies'—that is, sun, moon and stars—that modify etheric forces. The ethers, as universal forces, are not forces that shape form, but that dissolve it. They are not morphogenic or formative forces. Morphogenic forces arise when stellar influences work together with the ethers and modify their effect. Etheric morphogenic forces are therefore also peripheral forces; not universal ones however, not from the whole circumference, but rather from specific locations on the periphery, originating from the sun, the planets or other stars. They are *localized peripheral forces*. Just as the stars are continually in certain positions or moving in the heavens, so they are also continually modifying etheric forces, and no ether appears 'naked' in etheric space; it is always 'clothed' in a morphogenic force.

Before pursuing the question of whether stellar influences can also be found in the elements, we need first to interpolate a look at the origin of the elements themselves.

Elements are not forces. There are only two kinds of space: positive and negative. These are arenas of forces. There are three dimensions: three positive and three negative. There are four elements. The fiery element is without dimension; air is one-dimensional, water two-dimensional, and earth three-dimensional. These last three elements thereby integrate themselves into the dimensions of forces which are not their originators.

So where do elements originate? We can recall how, as described earlier [in Volume I], Aristotle taught Alexander the nature of the elements. He drew his attention to the cardinal points of the compass. What are cardinal points? They are facts associated with the horizon. Horizon means 'that which bounds or limits'. What is the horizon? It cannot be weighed or measured, yet it is a factor of the sense world with significant impact. It separates above and below, day and night, light and dark—similar to light, not as surface however, but as line. Growth and fall-lines are at right-angles to the earth's surface, with which they share a common point. The horizon also has a point in common with the surface of the earth. While this point lies on an ideal earth surface, i.e. on the surface of the ocean, the horizon is unborn. As soon as the point rises vertically above this base point, the horizon appears, and the point becomes its mid-point. The horizon can arise and disappear.

In order to see the horizon in its totality, this mid-point needs to move, to turn about itself. This is a non-spatial movement without a beginning or end in space. It is the movement of the fire-warmth-element, an intensive movement. Also belonging to this is the fact that time is manifested by the horizon. The sun rises over the horizon, appears, shines, is visible, then disappears again below the horizon. Arising, existing, and dying away in the sense world. No horizon: no time. The horizon is associated with the nature of warmth.

The horizon, divided into four quadrants, shows itself as the origin of the elements. The horizon is an earthly fact. It is the all-encompassing circumference. It always encircles the mid-point, without which it could not appear. But its power stretches even as far as the infinitely distant plane, as far as the vault of the heavens. It makes a part of the sky visible, and a part hidden. Every morning and evening the colours of twilight appear on the horizon and birdsong fills the air. In all this the horizon shows its power and nature as mid-point, just as the elements are the mid-point between the ethers and physical forces.

If we take seriously this way of looking at the horizon, we see it separates the world into an 'above' and 'below', into the visible and invisible. It separates the realms of form and substance. We only see the stars that are above the horizon, where they work in light. Below the horizon they work in darkness. Since the stars are constantly circling, they sometimes work *above*, sometimes *below* and sometimes *on* the horizon. If we look at the cosmos in the manner of modern mechanistic astronomy, this is meaningless. But it is not meaningless. For, sun and stars above the horizon and sun and stars below the horizon have a completely different effect on the real sense-perceptible world. The stars above the horizon—that is, during the day—work as shaping, *form-creating* forces, as do the movements of the planets at that time. At evening and morning, when the stars and planets are on the horizon, they work as *morphogenic forces of life*; their movements and harmonies of the spheres engender life and rhythm, create colour and sound. To the question as to how the stars work when they are below the horizon and work through the earth, we must answer: the same stars, when in darkness below the horizon, are *substance-forming* forces, they shape the interior matter that fills out and carries the external form. From the initially indefinite potential of the elements, stellar forces create specific substances. Stars are the originators of individual substances (this will be explored in greater detail later).

In his last Whitsun lecture, Rudolf Steiner describes the blue vault of heaven as the boundary of cosmic ether. The ether world reaches to the firmament, the sea of the four ethers. In its bosom it carries the four elements. The stars appear at the boundary of the firmament. The fixed stars are constant in their positions, the planets move with the sun in their cosmic harmonies. It is through these stars that the forces of spiritual beings penetrate the phenomenal world. They are astral and spiritual forces. When astral forces work through specific stellar regions (or worked through them in the Beginning), they stimulate the ethers and turn them into *etheric morphogenic forces*. Spiritual forces penetrate the earth more deeply, into the elements, and turn them into *elemental morphogenic forces*. Morphogenic *forces of life and rhythms* are generated in the circumference by the sun and its moving planets.[6]

Rudolf Steiner describes the totality of these forces as the Cosmic Word working in and through the stars. It is the *Logos* speaking, sounding, and contemplating through the stars. When it speaks from above through the stars, form-shaping forces arise; when it sings from the circumference, morphogenic forces of life arise; when it contemplates and generates through the earth from below, it creates morphogenic forces of substance (Diagram 2).

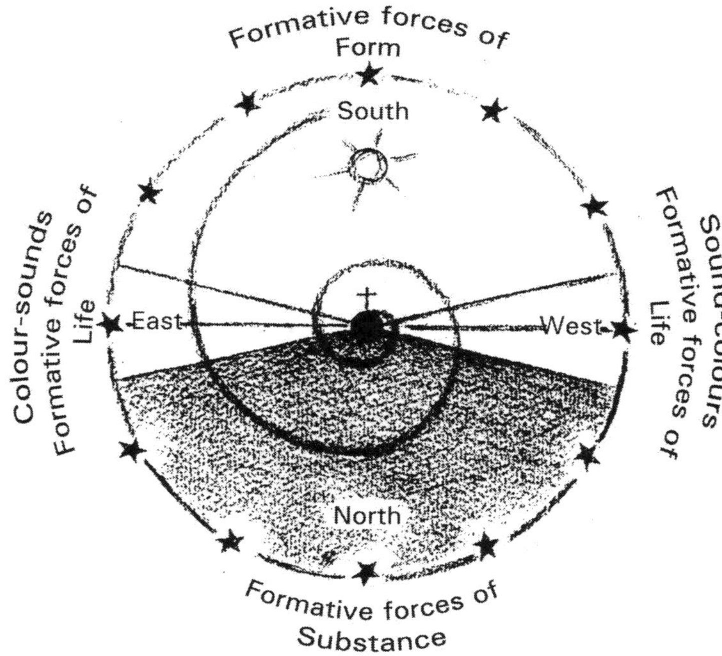

Diagram 2: Morphogenic forces and the Horizon

4. The Phenomenology of Etheric Formative or Morphogenic Forces

When we have a living organism before us—a plant, animal, or human being—we observe its surface, colour, shape, form. The limit of its body separates inner world from surrounding world. Without destroying the form we can only learn something about the organism's inner world by weighing it: its weight. When we destroy the inner and outer form—by eating the carrot or trout, or investigating the organism chemically or physically—we find its specific substance. Form and substance have come into being through life. Life has produced both. Put the other way round, it is in form and substance that active life processes take place.

We can thus distinguish three aspects in every living organism: its form, its life processes, its substance. All three arise as a result of life, through the etheric principle, through the etheric body. The etheric body must therefore contain the forces for all three: for the creation of form, the processes of life, the formation of substance. We will now describe these morphogenic forces in sequence.

Formative Forces of Shape or Form

> *'The etheric form becomes visible for us through the physical; but it is the etheric form that we actually see ...'*[7]

Growth Movement of Plants

In plants, the etheric predominates over the physical-earthly, so it is here that the etheric can be most easily studied. To begin with, our focus will be only on the processes creating form.

When we look at a plant—say, an annual flowering plant—and

the variety of forms in its stem, leaf, flower, etc., all that we see is the result of growth, i.e. from movement come to rest or with the appearance of rest. The effect of the growth process is that the plant, by striving upwards (expansion), simultaneously comes into its own proper form. Form is movement come to rest.

We will now look at plant forms and try to discover what movement has come to rest in each typical plant organ, that is, we will endeavour to distinguish specific individual movements within the total movement of growth. For this we will need to take into account the entire course of growth from the seed in the soil to the formation of new seed. (This method was used already in the Middle Ages by Albertus Magnus to investigate growth movements in plants.)

Characterizing movements in words can only be an approximation. This should be taken into account in the following descriptions, and the reader is called upon to complete, enliven and feel the descriptions from his own observation and experience.

1. The first thing the seed does in the earth is absorb moisture, strengthen its own inner force and *burst* the seed coat. It makes room for itself. This force is so great that in certain circumstances it *pushes aside* the surrounding earth. This first movement of growth is *germination.*
2. Immediately a new force comes into play: the seedling puts out a tiny root and begins to sprout, to grow upwards. *Sprouting* is a movement that enables the plant to push through the surface of the earth and *lift itself* above it. This is actually the primary force of the plant that is active throughout its growth, and which, overcoming the weight of earthly substances, carries it aloft. A matter-conquering force becomes visible in sprouting. This force lifts up into the vertical and is particularly clear in the upward-striving stem. It can be called *lifting, raising, sprouting.*
3. From here another force of movement emerges which no

longer lifts the growth process upward, but spreads it out into the horizontal, into breadth. Lateral swellings begin to form at the tip of the stem, the growth point, which open out as leaves. The plant starts to leaf. What was lifted up in sprouting now, in leaf-formation, flows sideways into a form, fills out the form and then stops, comes to rest. *Spreading, unfolding.*

4. As the ascending sprouting continues, it is as though it meets an obstruction, it *blocks* and *stalls*. While the ascending stream continues to push against this *obstruction* which persists, the buds begin now to form in a distinct growth movement of their own. So, *bud formation.*
5. Looking at a plant in the budding stage—at a rose bush or a chestnut bud—one has the impression that the bud is encased, enfolded. A protective layer encloses it. This impression extends over the whole plant, and one notices that the entire green plant is as though enveloped in a skin. This skin sets boundaries to all movements of growth, protects and individualizes the plant being: *protective layer, covering with a skin.*
6. Now, there are plants that do not send all their forces into the leaf form or the resting bud: the grapevine for example, or the pea, forms a threadlike stalk, a tendril. This exhibits a circular movement that continues until the tendril finds something to cling to, and then it contracts and holds on in a tight spiral. There are plants which form tendrils, but others where the whole plant twines, as in beans and creepers. The possibility for this kind of movement is hidden in every plant. Even where it does not show outwardly, it is active in all plants in the formation of spiral cells (*Spiralzellen*). These make it possible for the plant to sway. Without flexibility or the ability to bend in response to wind or touch, and then come upright again, the plant could not exist. Yielding and self-assertion! But also, in the bud, the petals are rolled up, crumpled and waiting to unroll. So *winding, swaying, rolling.*

7. The bud is only a temporary block in the movement; then the movement continues. The bud swells, opens and blossoms: *opening, blossoming.*
8. A part of the flower petal rolls up to form the thread-thin stamens which, from the anthers, release their contents of pollen grains into the atmosphere. The plant releases pollen, scent, and streams out. So, *releasing pollen.*

At this juncture the plant has come to a certain conclusion. The upward-thrusting growth force, the plant's urge to lift itself out of the earth and expand, has attained its goal, indeed it has even overshot the mark by losing itself in formlessness, in pollen and scent, in the atmosphere. The plant's life appears to have come to an end.

9. Now something surprising happens: a growth force from above downwards. A grain of pollen falls on the stigma, and the pollen tube grows downwards to the ovary. The result is fertilization, the germ of a new plant has arisen: *receiving, fertilization, fructification.*
10. The growth force accumulates nutrients around the germ. The seed embryos begin to form, the enveloping layer around the seed fills out, and fruit forms: *fruiting.*
11. When ears of corn hang low with grain, when apples weigh down the branches, the plant unburdens itself of the weight, casts it off, and actively throws off what has become heavy: *dropping fruit, unburdening, lightening.*
12. The plant has brought forth seeds for a new plant, and a final force now causes the plant in its form to rigidify. All movement comes to a halt and ceases. Now in the fields we see stubble, dry umbels, rigid husks. Even the seed is dry, rigid, durable and lasting: *drying out, rigidifying.*

Putting these growth movements or morphogenic forces together, one gets the following order of eight ascending and four descending movements of growth:

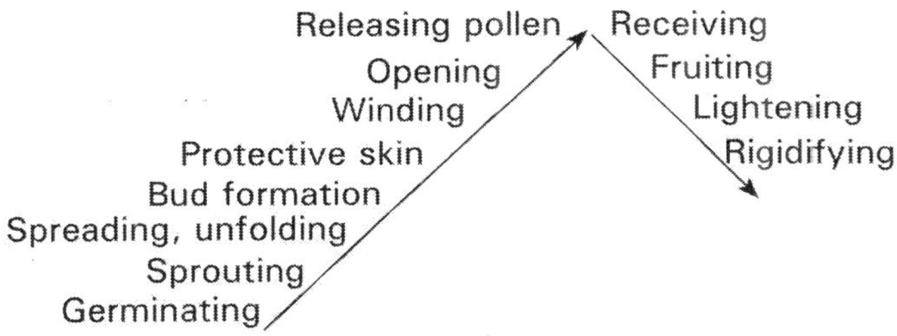

Initially, twelve distinct movements of growth can be differentiated in the growth of the plant. Later more will be added. We must be clear about the nature of these growth forces. They are forces of building up, of life in the plant, in other words, of its etheric body. They are peripheral forces working as negative space from the surroundings and shaping the plant's form.

When we see a plant growing, we should not imagine that it is pushed up out of the earth from below. There is no force in the earth that pushes up earthly matter and at the same time gives it shape.

It is etheric morphogenic forces that exert an upward-drawing, 'suctional' effect on the germinating seeds and in this drawing-up create the movements and forms described above. The effects of etheric morphogenic forces become visible to our sensory perception in the forms of plants. Morphogenic forces in themselves are supersensible and cannot be physically perceived. Nevertheless, through observation and thinking—or, as Goethe said, 'with contemplative discernment'—they can be characterized as twelve distinct movements of growth.

Comparison of Movements of Growth with Movements of Eurythmy

Now we can ask: Can these twelve morphogenic forces be found anywhere other than in the shaping of plants? Are there movements in other circumstances that can be compared with the above movements of growth?

Rudolf Steiner researched the facts here and presented them as follows:

- Morphogenic forces can be perceived by a clairvoyant investigator in the life-organism of every living thing; hence the alternative term, 'body of formative forces'.
- These formative forces are active in the sounds of human speech.

Regarding this last point, the sounds of speech, combined in the alphabet, are the same for all human beings. For every sound there is a characteristic position of the organs of articulation (larynx, lips, tongue, palate, etc.). In speaking, forms arise in the air that are a manifestation of morphogenic forces. These airy speech sounds however are so fleeting that they are imperceptible, or can only be studied with special technical apparatus.[8]

However, for an investigator able to perceive supersensibly, there is another possibility for direct perception of these morphogenic forces of speech. When someone *listens* to speech or music, something else is also happening: forms arise in his etheric body that correspond to the sounds of speech or musical tones. In this way Rudolf Steiner was able to investigate the movement gestures for each individual sound of speech, and for each note and musical element (intervals, major and minor keys, etc.). It was this set of laws that became the foundation for eurythmy.[9]

Eurythmy is a new art of movement created by Rudolf Steiner, which can therefore also be called visible speech and visible song. The person doing eurythmy carries out movements with his whole body—predominantly with arms and hands—which are made by his own etheric body in the act of listening. In his eurythmic movements he thereby brings to manifestation through the visible body the otherwise invisible inner etheric movements of formative forces.

Now we find something very surprising and revealing: we rediscover the movements of eurythmy in the growth movements of plants. Indeed, the forces of growth and form in every living organism are the same as the eurythmic gestures of speech and music, in other words, the movements of eurythmy are what constitute the body of morphogenic forces—they are the formative forces of the cosmos.

We could also say: as it grows, the plant does eurythmy. To be convinced of this one would need to know the movements of eurythmy and compare them with movements of growth. This is difficult today because very few people—least of all scientists—are familiar with eurythmy. An artistic, inwardly resonating feeling for form is also necessary. Nevertheless we will look at the characteristics of eurythmic movements as researched by Rudolf Steiner, place them alongside growth movements of the plant, and compare them.[10*]

1. Germinating corresponds eurythmically to G (or K). It is a pushing-away movement, a pressing outwards so that the essence can emerge. G masters matter from out of the spirit.
2. Sprouting corresponds to L. L is the creative, morphogenic principle in all things and beings; it is the power of form overcoming matter.
3. Spreading, unfolding corresponds to M. M causes matter to flow into the leaf form, it has something about it that is open to approaching everything, that warmly touches and takes on the form of everything, is accommodating to everything.
4. Bud formation corresponds to N. N is a movement of sensing or perceiving that then jerks back, where something is dammed up, blocked.
5. Forming an enveloping layer corresponds to V [German: W]. The wave movement of V gives a boundary and envelops the whole plant like a skin.

---

[*] Translator's note: It is important in what follows to be aware that the letter for the consonants stands for the *sound* that it represents, and not the *name* of the letter, so without any accompanying vowel sound. For example, M represents the sound 'mmm', and not 'em' which is its name and a combination of two sounds: 'e' and 'm'. Likewise L represents the sound 'lll' and not 'el', etc.

6. Winding corresponds to R [i.e. a trilled, rolled R produced by a fluttering of the tip of the tongue, not a guttural or English R]. The plant's turning movement in winding and swaying in the wind is the rolling movement of R.
7. Blossoming corresponds to H; it is that which wafts towards one. The breath-sound H is found in the opening of the bud, in the unfolding of the blossom, in becoming airy.
8. Releasing pollen corresponds to F. The releasing and floating of pollen is like the breath-sound F, a pushing-out, blowing-away movement.
9. Receiving, pollination is T (D). Receiving pollen that grows down the style to fertilize the ovary is T; that which is weighty and important, even creative, and streams to earth from heaven; streams down with significance from above.
10. Fruiting: B. Fruit formation consists of enveloping the seed embryo with a nurturing layer, just as B in eurythmy is a nurturing, enfolding, protecting movement.
11. Lightening [release of a weight] is C [this is the German C which sounds similar to 'ts']. C [ts] is a becoming-lighter as when the seed pops lightly away, or the branch swings up again when the heavy fruits drop.
12. Rigidifying is S. The cessation of all movement, whereby the form becomes rigid and fixed, is the eurythmic movement of S, a movement that commands all motion to a standstill and rest. It also has something frightening about it, against which one must guard oneself.

In summary we have:

Germinating = G (K)	Blossoming = H
Sprouting = L	Releasing pollen = F
Spreading, unfolding = M	Receiving, pollination = T (D)
Damming up = N	Fruiting = B
Forming an envelope = V	Lightening = C ['ts']
Winding, twining = R	Rigidifying = S (Z)

In this way we find twelve *consonantal* sound-movements in the formation of the plant. But what are we to make of this?

Origin of Eurythmic Formative Forces in the Constellations

When eurythmy is done it requires a speaker to speak the sounds, the language, so that the eurythmist can represent them in his or her movements. With the plants there is no such speaker—or is there? If there is, then it is a language we cannot hear with our ears! It is the language of the *cosmic Word*. The cosmic Word speaks, the plant 'hears' it, 'eurythmizes' it and forms its shape.

Where does the cosmic Word sound? It is true that St John's Gospel opens with 'In the Beginning was the Word ... and without Him was not anything made that was made.' But today this Word is not regarded as a fact or concept of science. Anthroposophical spiritual science differs here, and describes how the cosmic Word, the Logos, manifests itself in the realities of the world and of man, and in nature. The cosmic Word is evident in a wonderful way in the starry heavens.

Where does the speaking of the cosmic Word come from for the plant? From the stars, through which the Logos speaks, stimulating the sea of ethers and shaping them into differentiated forces of form. Formative, morphogenic forces are peripheral forces, whose origin is a specific location in the circumference, a star or constellation. Their origin is actually astral in nature. Thus the ether space between heaven and earth is filled with etheric morphogenic forces shaped by the stars, and containing the potential for every possible shape and form.

Rudolf Steiner investigated the origin of speech sounds in the periphery and, for consonants, found it in the twelve forces of the zodiac. These are also the origin of the growth movements of plants. The sounds are attributed to the zodiac in the following order:

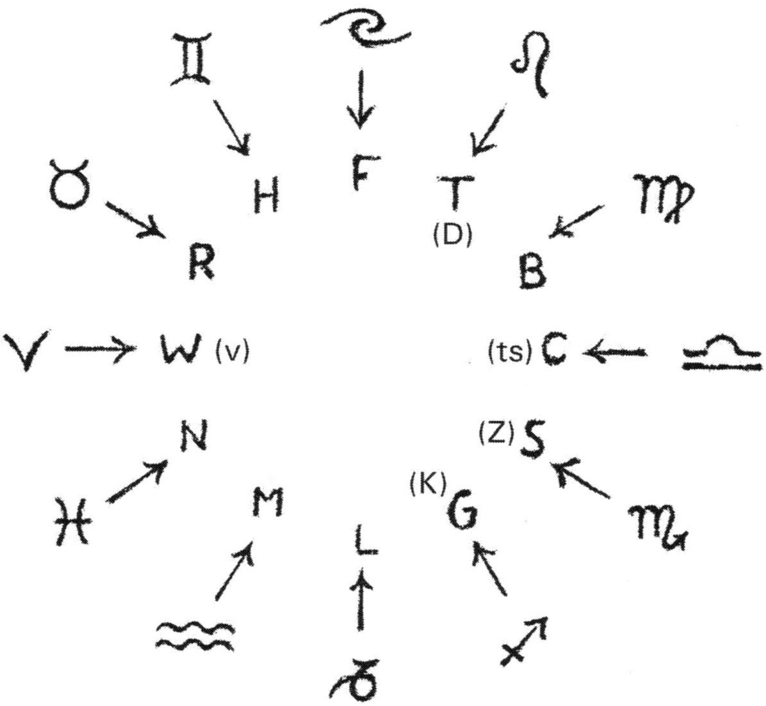

Diagram 3: The zodiac as origin of consonantal morphogenic forces

When we arrange the growth movements of plants through the zodiac according to the course of the year, we find that the life cycle of the plant corresponds to the cycle of the year (see Diagram 4). It begins in Sagittarius and finishes in Scorpio. In the period before Christmas, the plant-being imbues itself in the seed or leaf-bud with forces of germination. This agrees with botanical knowledge which has found that the first stirrings of life in the plant occur in December. In our latitudes, many plants actually need a period of winter frost before the sprouting and shooting begins in the spring. Colourful flowering begins around Whitsun, the plant ripens and bears fruit in the warmth of autumn, and is finished with the storms of November.

When we experience in this way the development of the plant through the course of the year, we can present the working together of morphogenic forces with ethers and elements in the

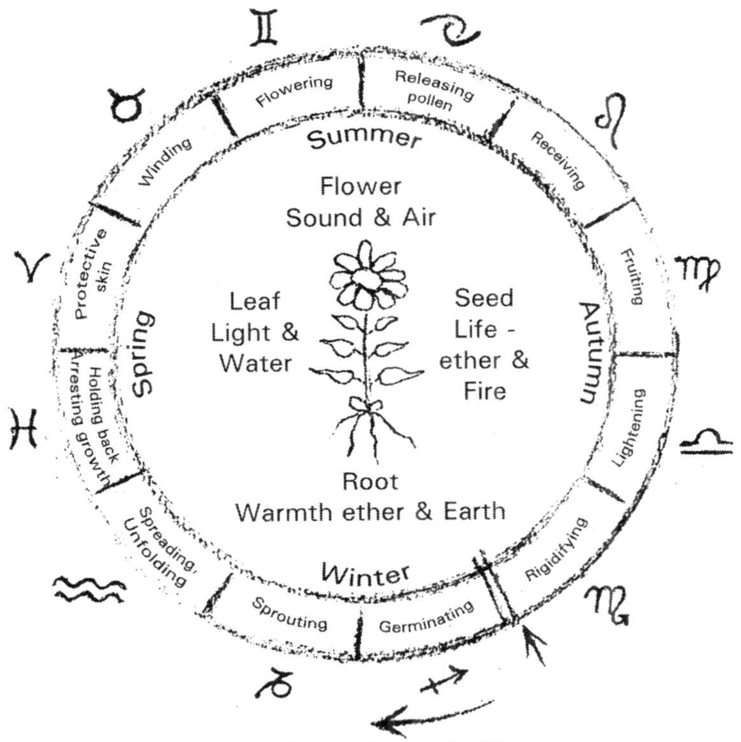

Diagram 4: Plant life in the course of the year

main organs of the plant as follows: In the root during winter's cold morphogenic forces take hold particularly of warmth-ether in the earth-element; towards spring the morphogenic forces work in the region of stem and leaf through light-ether in water-element; in summer they shape flowers in the air-element through the sound/chemical-ether; and in autumn the fruits and seeds are ripened through life-ether in warmth (see Diagram 5).

The twelve movements of growth we looked at above correspond to the twelve consonants of the zodiac. In spoken language there are more than twelve consonants, but these are simply modifications of those we have considered, and belong to the relevant constellation. Thus g and k, t and d, b and p, s and z belong together.

But language doesn't consist only of consonants—it also has vowels. Are there also vocalic formative forces? Does the cosmic Word also speak vowels to the plants? Yes indeed: the eurythmic vowels are also to be found in plant growth.

In order to find them, we'll approach this the other way round—we'll start with the vowels and look for their correspondence in the plant.

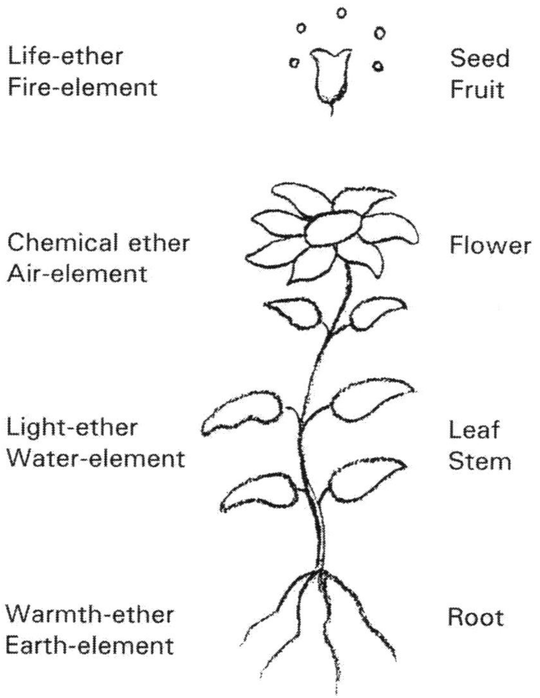

Diagram 5: Working together of ethers and elements in the plant

In eurythmy, the vowel movements are done with the arms as follows:*

A ['ah' /a:/] reaches out with open arms in an angle towards the periphery, as though towards two stars;

E ['eh' /e:/] is a holding oneself firmly in the crossing point of crossed arms;

---

*Translator's note: Vowels and diphthongs are given below as in the German original, followed by an English approximation and the IPA representation.

I ['ee' /i:/]	is a straight stretching [of one arm] upwards and [the other arm] downwards, like the axis in a spinning globe;
O ['oh' /o:/]	is a round, lovingly embracing, enclosing movement;
U ['oo' /u:/]	arms are straight and parallel, almost touching each other;
Ei ['eye' /aɪ/]	is a movement where one arm, as in E, glides and strokes along the other which is held straight as in I ['ee'];
Au ['ow' /au/]	is a half 'A' with one arm while the other touches the body.

Rudolf Steiner also investigated the cosmic origin of the vowels. It is in the planets.[11] Sun and Moon are included with the wandering stars. We find the following order (see next page).

So where in the plant are the vocalic morphogenic forces to be found that come from the planets? Whereas consonantal morphogenic forces, working alone or jointly, bring forth all possible forms and morphologies, the planetary morphogenic forces build the *structure* and *overall shape* of the plant.

A look at the form and structure of a plant shows that actually all plants have an axis around which everything is arranged and turns. This is the formative force of I ['ee'].

The plant spreads out up to a certain limit, giving it its *silhouette,* and the growth forces maintain this limit, even regenerating it when, for example, the tip is broken off in a storm. Every tree can be recognized at a distance by its silhouette. It is the force that lovingly delimits the plant: the vowel O.

While O forms the plant's widest expanse, there is another force that as though compresses it. It forms stem and trunk, leafstalk, needles, and everything that is narrow and firm in the plant. This is U ['oo'] (clearly experienced in a high pine forest with its tall parallel trunks).

Then there is a force that divides and forks stem and trunk,

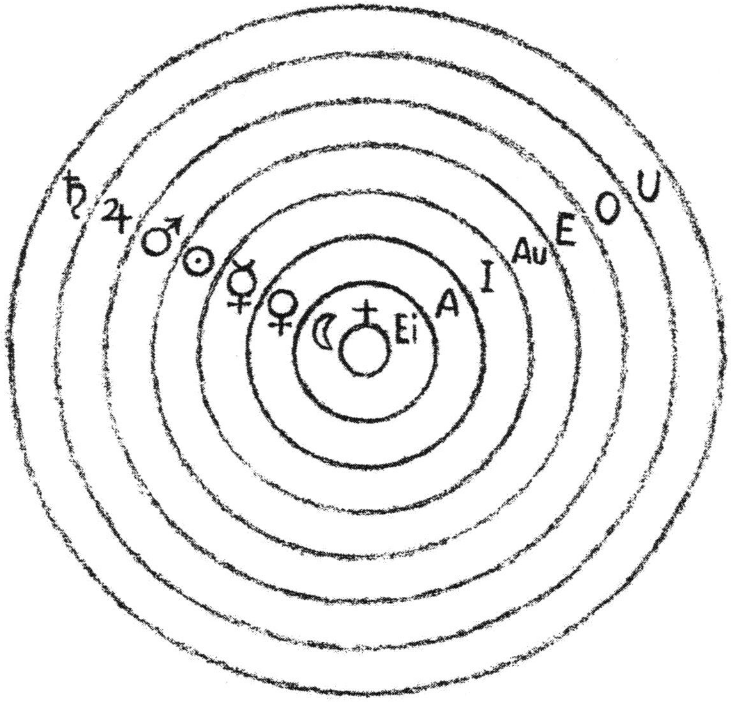

A	Venus		
E	Mars	AU	Sun
I	Mercury		
O	Jupiter	EI	Moon
U	Saturn		

Diagram 6: Planetary spheres with vowels

separates into twigs and branches, *creates angles*. This is A ['ah'].

In the crossing between leaf-shoot and stem, the *bud* arises in the leaf axis—E ['eh'].

EI ['eye'] is the E that *stops the ascent* of I. The spiralling leaf arrangement no longer moves upwards but circles at the same level, giving rise to the flower and later the ovaries. Eichendorff expresses this in his poem *Mondnacht* [Moonlit night]: 'It was as though the sky / had gently kissed the earth / so that in a haze of blossom / she now dreamed of him.'

AU is the expression of the whole plant, extension and contraction, which Goethe recognized as being the essential nature of the archetypal plant. It is as though the sun intones three times its call, AU, and with it numerous shaping forces of the planets and fixed stars step into action, causing the archetypal plant to manifest in its threefold metamorphosis in every plant formation perceptible to the senses.

Just as for Goethe the archetypal plant was 'the result of living experience', so the morphogenic consonant and vowel forces of the archetypal plant can also be 'the result of living experience' for the observer schooled in eurythmy. What Goethe, in respect of the archetypal plant's metamorphosis of shape, could only differentiate as threefold expansion and contraction, and what enabled him to experience that 'the whole plant is actually leaf'—eurythmically a threefold A U M—can be experienced today in detail in the shaping forces of its form.

Tonal Formative/Morphogenic Forces

But the form of the plant is not yet complete. What is still missing is everything that can be morphologically counted and measured, everything that is rhythmical: the angle of the axial buds, the distances between them, the numbers in a diagram of a flower and in the spirals of leaves. There are plants whose branches go out horizontally, in others they point steeply upwards or droop down. All these phenomena, which can be enumerated and measured, are the elements of tone eurythmy in the plant. There is enormous potential here for future research.

Since the eurythmic formative forces of tone also originate in the the cosmos, particularly in the rhythms of the sun and planets, future musicians and astronomers will need to work together with botanists and organic chemists—something that already happens in anthroposophical research.[12]

Here we can draw attention most especially to the research results of Ernst-Michael Kranich in which, using a Goethean scientific approach, the form and growth movements of plants are compared with the cosmic rhythms and paths of the planets.[13] Kranich, through a 'correspondence of images', brings us to the view that each plant family is a *type* connected with an individual planet. Whereas through speech eurythmy we experienced the archetypal plant's sculpted form, Kranich's research leads beyond this to an experience of the 'type' permeated by mobile musicality:

> For we become evermore clearly aware that the entire planetary world reveals itself in individual plant genera, and in such a way that its rhythms and spheres penetrate with varying intensity. We experience the individual plant as a mighty musical chord in which separate notes sound in varying rhythms and intensity.[14]

The following diagrams, shown by kind permission of the publisher Verlag Freies Geisteleben, can encourage us to look at the correspondence of images and read Kranich's book in the original.

Rudolf Steiner created eurythmy as an art form; but art is a manifestation of hidden laws in nature. When Steiner writes of Goethe: 'Goethe sought to unite with the cosmic spirit and to reveal its power and workings; he did this through the medium of art or science, as required'[15]—this also applies in large measure to Steiner himself. In eurythmy Steiner created a key to understanding morphogenic forces. Eurythmy, in speech eurythmy and tone eurythmy, makes speech sounds and musical notes visible, it is visible speech and visible music.

Just as in Diagrams 3 and 6 we indicated the cosmic origin of speech sounds [i.e. the zodiac], so the origin of musical notes and intervals can be given as the planets, with the zodiac as the origin for the circle of keys (circle of fifths/fourths). This is shown in the following two diagrams.

Planets in order of distance from earth, and their corresponding musical note:

Saturn	–	G	Mercury	–	D
Jupiter	–	E	Venus	–	F
Mars	–	C	Moon	–	B
Sun	–	A			

Diagram 7: Geocentric path of Venus with 'Venus flowers'

The intervals are hidden in the stages of evolution:

Saturn – Tonic
Sun – Second
Moon – augmented and diminished Third
Mars – Fourth
Mercury – Fifth
Jupiter – Sixth
Venus – Seventh
Vulcan – Octave

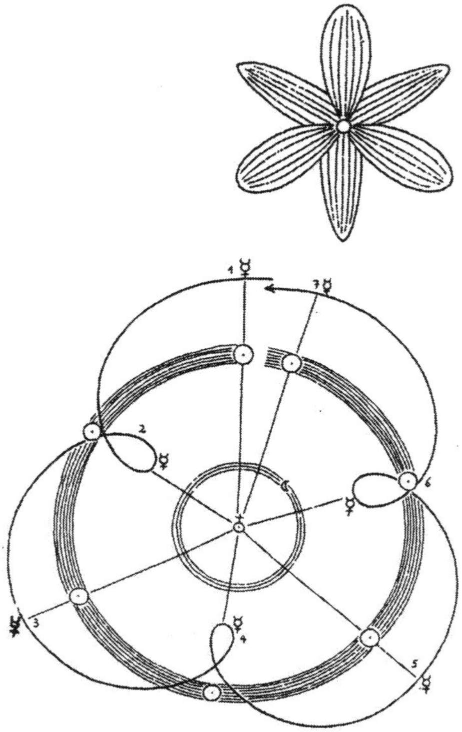

Diagram 8: Geocentric path of Mercury with tulip flower

Formative Forces of Colour

When eurythmy as an art form is performed on stage, it is undulating, moving colour. Steiner designed two-dimensional figures for most of the speech sounds showing statically the characteristic movement-form of each, and also the corresponding colours. In a performance of Steiner's work *Zwölf Stimmungen* [Twelve Moods], in which the twelve signs of the zodiac and the seven planets appear, the whole world of colour is presented in its connection with the cosmos.

This brings us back to our initial question as to the quality of red, and we can now say: behind colour there are also cosmic formative forces which have their origin in the heavenly bodies. Diagrams 3 and 6, shown in this book [Volume 1] in black-and-white, are based on colours according to Steiner's indications.

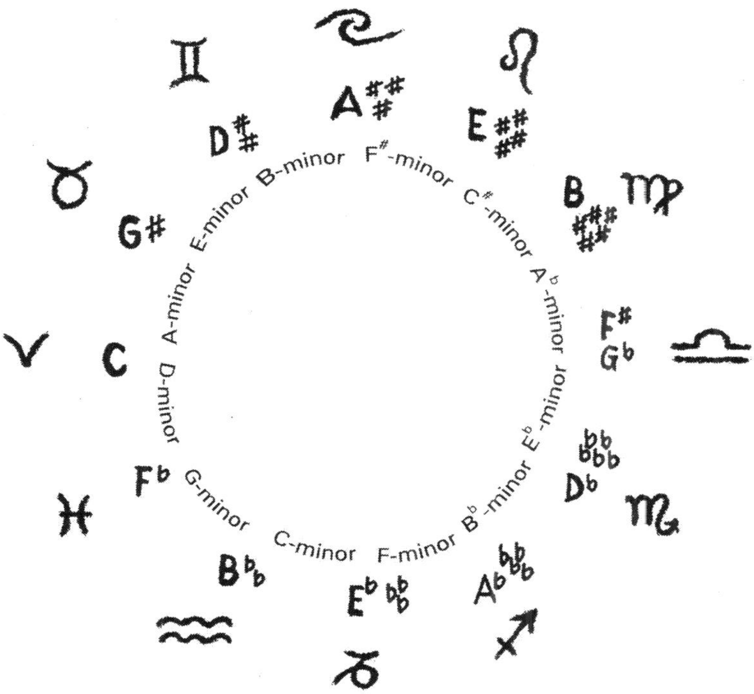

Diagram 9: Circle of Musical Keys in the Zodiac

What we experience as red is a cosmic 'formative-force-of-red', and this red-forming force reveals the feeling of the World Soul, of the Logos.

A full presentation of the colour- and tone-formative forces will hopefully be possible sometime in the future. Some beautiful beginnings have already been made towards this in the work of many anthroposophical authors.

Practical Consequences

Seventy-five years of research into morphogenic forces in all areas of anthroposophically oriented natural science have advanced our understanding, particularly in biology, medicine, pharmacy, hydrology and agriculture. With regard to practical image-forming methods, we can mention Pfeiffer's capilliary dynamolysis (*Steigbilder*) and blood crystallization methods [e.g.

copper chloride crystallization of blood samples for diagnostic purposes], as well as Schwenk's drop-image method for testing the quality of water.

From the abundance of new research results, we will look at their application in two areas, agriculture and medicine, which have proven their usefulness.

Seed-sowing Days according to Maria Thun

In his *Agriculture Course*, Rudolf Steiner points out that already in ancient India seed was sown according to the phases of the moon as happens still today, for example in Yemen.[16] According to Lili Kolisko, the horticulturist Maria Thun decided to pursue this further. In doing so she made a discovery of the greatest importance for human nutrition.[17] Over decades of research she traced the influence of zodiacal forces on plant growth, and learnt how to manage these for practical use. Certain times became apparent that were favourable for development of the various parts of the plant such as root, stem/leaf, flower, seed/fruit. This is particularly important for food crops where we are dealing with a one-sided development of the edible product of the plant, e.g. root (carrots, radishes, parsnips, celeriac), stem/leaf (asparagus, lettuce, cabbage, spinach, rhubarb), flower (cauliflower, broccoli), and seed/fruit (grains, apples, berries, peas, beans).

A connection could be seen between the sidereal moon cycle and the zodiac. The moon is the mediator of morphogenic forces from the zodiac. In the inorganic realm this can also be seen in the sand forms on the beach after ebb tide—characteristic recurring patterns arise in the sand depending on the position of the moon in a particular constellation of the zodiac.[18]

For plant growth, Maria Thun's investigations indicated the following: when the moon is in a particular region of the zodiac, it mediates particularly strongly the forces of that constellation to the plant. When seed is sown on that day and the earth cultivated, there is benefit from the constellations for a particular part of the plant. Root growth is promoted by Taurus, Virgo and Capricorn; leaf and stem are promoted by Cancer, Scorpio and Pisces; flower formation is promoted by Gemini, Libra and Aquarius; fruit and seed are promoted by Leo, Sagittarius and Aries. In this last group it is particularly clear that as the moon passes through Leo, not only is fruit formation promoted, but also especially the quality of the seed.

These zodiacal regions give us four possible trigons in the zodiac, as shown in Diagram 10.

Ever since ancient times people have known that forces in the the zodiac are connected with the four elements, and a trigon was identified for each of them – an earthy, watery, airy and fiery trigon. In the plant, the elements are active in ascending order in root, leaf, flower and fruit. So when in the zodiac the moon is in an earth constellation, the plant is particularly stimulated in its

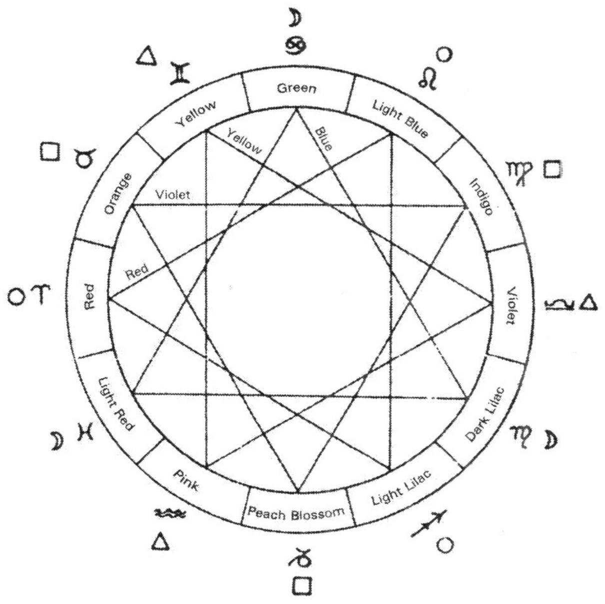

Earth	□:	violet trigon	Air	△:	yellow trigon
Water	☽:	blue trigon	Fire	○:	red trigon

Diagram 10: The Four Zodiacal Trigons

'earthy region', in other words in its root formation, and likewise with the other element trigons.

Maria Thun's planting and sowing calendar is essentially based on these connections, and its application in horticulture and agriculture has already led to impressive results.

Building on Thun's understanding of trigon influences and the connection of the trigons with root, leaf, flower and fruit, we can go more deeply into these parts of the plant by taking into account not only the effect of the element but also of the morphogenic forces active in the separate points of the trigon. We then find archetypes as it were of the four parts of the plant, whose genesis can be experienced in its cosmic relationships:

Earth Trigon

Root formation by

Taurus	– Virgo	– Capricorn
Twining/creeping	– Fruiting	– Sprouting
R	– B	– L

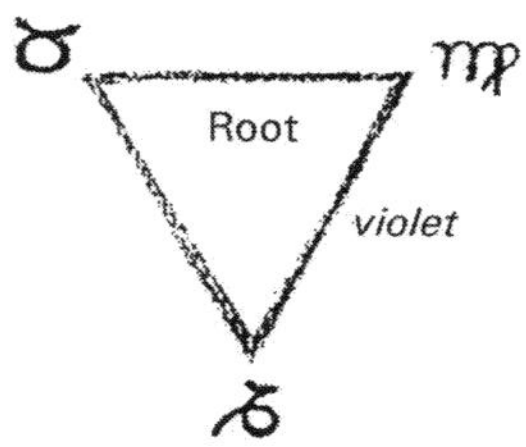

Diagram 11

The root seeks to get a firm hold of the earth by sending out its side shoots. Sprouting at germination is the main service the root performs for the plant's existence. Fruiting in the root means accumulating and storing nutrients, growing thick and round.

Water Trigon

Leaf formation by

Pisces	– Cancer	– Scorpio
Holding back	– Pollinating	– Rigidifying
N	– F	– S

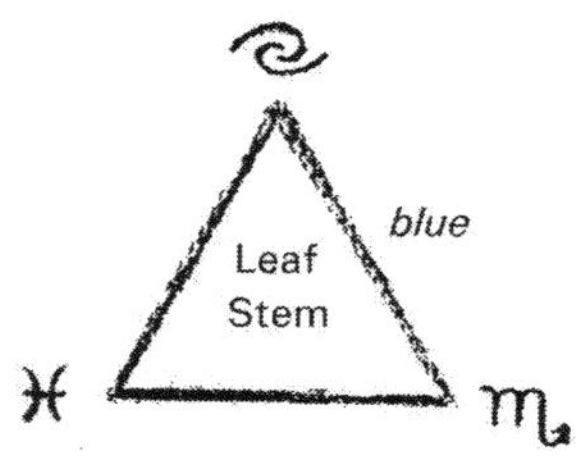

Diagram 12

Leaf buds and cabbage heads are formed by a process of damming up, holding back. Stamens are rolled up leaves. Once the leaf has formed it can then rigidify—that is, hold its form—for the whole plant is actually leaf.

Air Trigon

Flower formation by

Aquarius	– Gemini	– Libra
Growing shoots	– Opening	– Lightening
M	– H	– C [ts]

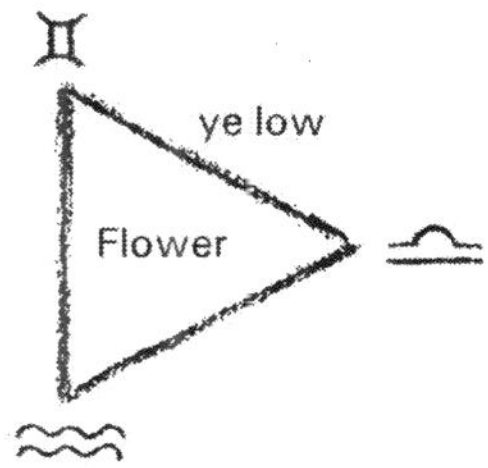

Diagram 13

Putting out leaf-shoots is growth into the horizontal, which is most radically realized in the flower. Flowering is an opening, unfolding. The flower of the cauliflower becomes heavy, otherwise the petals drop.

Fire Trigon

Fruit/seed formation by

Leo	– Aries	– Sagittarius
Receiving	– Enfolding	– Germinating
T	– V	– K

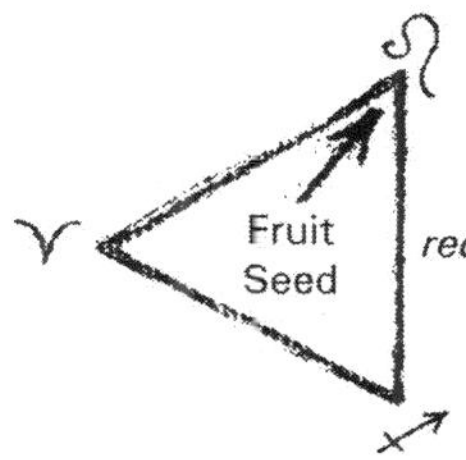

Diagram 14

The formative force of Leo is that of fertilizing, receiving. The seedling is the start of a new individual plant. This needs a strong coat to survive the winter. Then the germinating power must burst the coat and release the new plant into the world. Maria Thun's research has shown that the best seeds develop in the constellation of Leo, which is understandable for it is here that the seedling arises.

With research into morphogenic forces, and practical experimentation such as that carried out by Maria Thun and others, we can hope that a future can be found for the dying plant life of the earth by mobilizing forces that are connected to the cosmos.

Curative Eurythmy / Eurythmy Therapy

The division of nature into four kingdoms arises from the addition of consciousness in animal and man, and of self-consciousness in man. In spiritual science the forces creating consciousness and self-consciousness are termed respectively 'astrality' and 'spirit'. The plant has only the physical and etheric principles. Thus in spiritual science the kingdoms of nature are differentiated according to the four components of being: the mineral is purely earthly-physical; the plant has a physical and an etheric body; the animal additionally has an astral body; and man has an I-organization, 'I' or Ego.

The real inner life in animal and man is not only expressed in consciousness and self-consciousness; it also creates for itself an inner life in the body, which is lacking in plants. The possibility for this arises from a growth principle that is absent in plants.

From the point of the seed, the plant grows into the space of light, i.e. it extends the soil's realm of darkness, to which as root it belongs, by lifting up earthly substances through the forces of growth, and filling out its form, created by etheric morphogenic forces, with this earthly matter. This is why, for example, a tree trunk can be described as raised up earth [or, more strictly, raised up humus]. This attachment to the ground also prevents the plant from moving freely over the earth.

Now in the animal something completely unexpected happens: it creates its own realm of darkness into which it grows. This is made possible by the inward folding that is known in science as *gastrulation*. The process of gastrulation is as follows: the fertilized animal ovum divides into smaller and smaller cells that form the wall of a fluid-filled bladder, the *blastula*. On a certain point the blastula indents and folds inwards by invaginaton into a cup-shape which, by further growth, finally forms a tube-like inner structure. Thus is formed the primitive gut and mouth.

What is the significance of this infolding? This event contains cosmic mysteries. Gastrulation brings about a separation of the world into outer and inner worlds. The plant does not yet divide the world. It leaves the separation of light-filled upper realm and dark subterranean realm as it is, and participates in both. The animal separates off from the world. It becomes its own miniature world which can move over the greater one.

We can ask: What is it that the animal infolds into itself? And we have to answer: The animal infolds the plant into itself, and man additionally infolds the mineral. The wall of the invaginated primitive gut, which in the course of animal evolution becomes increasingly differentiated and complex, and in human development appears as the endoderm, is like the surface of the earth which has up-building forces above and breaking-down forces below. Within the gut (lumen) are the forces of break-down, and outside it, directed towards the body, are the up-building forces where the animal astral forces—and in man also the I-organization—structure the body. For this they employ the formative forces of the infolded plant, forming from them the organs of the endodermic metabolic region. In this way a structure 'sprouts' from the gut wall which in external nature would become a plant, but in the animal and human inner world becomes the organ protrusions of the primitive gut and endoderm. In this way, going from top to bottom, the glands are formed (pituitary, salivary); the lungs; the extended stomach and gastric juice glands; the liver-spleen-pancreas glandular system with formation of the gall bladder; the convoluting of the intestines with their enormous surface area and countless digestive glands; the formation of the bladder, etc. We can therefore say that, in the structure of their organs, man and animal have internalized the world of morphogenic forces which, in the plant, still shape it directly from the cosmos. At first sight there is no apparent similarity between human or animal organs, and plant forms. Only when we are in a position to investigate the morphogenic etheric processes behind them does the connection emerge. It thus becomes clear that this inner world is founded on the activity of formative forces. What is hidden in the human body is revealed in the plant. I look at the plant, see its movements of growth, and it reveals what occurs in man.

In this context new possibilities arise in therapy for working directly on the inner formation of the organism using movement exercises. The movements of eurythmy in particular can have a strengthening effect on the internal organism. These therapeutic possibilities are the basis of the curative eurythmy [or eurythmy therapy] given by Rudolf Steiner.[19] This is a mode of treatment which has long since proven itself in anthroposophical medicine as a rational new approach.

It is neither possible nor our task here to describe in detail the efficacy of eurythmy therapy. Only a few indications will be described in connection with the 'infolded plant'. For this we can imagine the human being as an inverted plant with root formation in the brain and nervous sphere, stem and leaf formation in the middle respiratory-circulatory system, and the flower in the metabolic-sexual system.

Ingested food mass is held back in the stomach as in a bud. The passage out of the stomach opens rhythmically allowing only an appropriate amount of chyme to pass through. In cases of disturbed pylorus function, the curative eurythmy H-movement is helpful, corresponding to opening. With accelerated bowel passage and tendency to diarrhoea, the N-movement, the movement of damming up, is effective. With spastic constipation and irregular restricted bowel movement (*Colitis irritabile*) the curative eurythmy R-sound is helpful for regularizing bowel movement and peristalsis.

The interior of the gut is the arena of forces that break down. But just as these forces [in external nature], by means of bacteria, create soil humus from which the root derives the substances with which the plant forms its structure, so the intestinal villi extend into the digested content of the intestines, extract nutrients from it, and convey these to the lymph and blood. If the process of absorption is too weak, it can be strengthened by the L-movement. L is the force that lifts substance into levity and leads it into the flows of life. Just as AU ['ow'] appears as the expression of the whole plant in its expansion and contraction, so the curative eurythmy AU, or the whole sequence of vowels from A to U, works on the circulation, on the flowing together and separating of numerous fluids. M, which corresponds to leaf formation in the plant, stimulates overall respiration in the human being including the inner respiration of cells, and strengthens exhalation.

These few examples show how a connection can be found

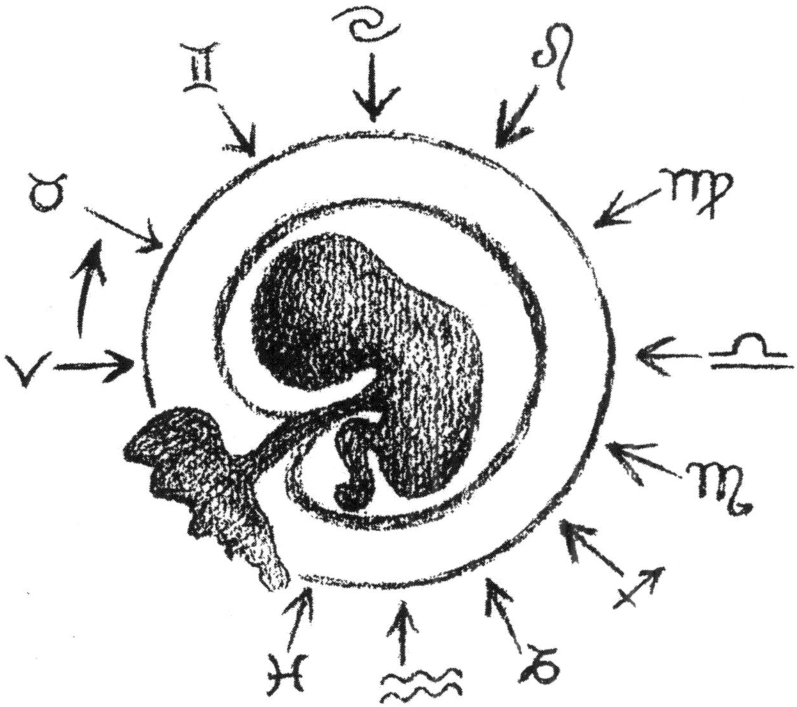

Diagram 15: The shaping of the outer human form from the zodiac, in the embryo

between organic processes and the movements of eurythmy, or conversely from the movements to the organism and physiology, when we are acquainted with the formative forces.

In order to study curative eurythmy today at special training institutions, a full eurythmy training is first required. Eurythmy therapists, who are also required to have a sufficient grounding in the principles of medicine, treat patients in collaboration with a doctor.

In Goethe's day the principle of infolding (gastrulation), which

Diagram 16: Fifteenth century woodcut showing the shaping of the human form by the Zodiac in a standing figure

constitutes a fundamental distinction between plants and animals, was not yet known. Goethe was therefore unable to elaborate the idea of the archetypal animal (*Urtier*) in the same way as he did for the archetypal plant (*Urpflanze*).

The outer form of man and animal also has its origin in the zodiac—but in a new act of creation, as it were. The genesis of the plant form, once the seedling has burst the seed coat, takes place in light-filled regions of the earth; the genesis of the human form takes place in a space of darkness enveloped in embryonic sheaths in the mother's body. The growing form lies rolled up in a kind of spherical envelope. The zodiacal forces act in cyclical sequence. In the plant, as mentioned earlier, formative-force activity begins with Sagittarius and ends with Scorpio. In man, the shaping of the outer form begins in Aries, with the formation of the brow and cranium, and ends in Pisces with the feet. Medieval pictures still show a knowledge of this (see Diagram 16).

Formative Forces of Life

The formative forces for life processes will now be described according to the morphogenic forces that constitute the body of formative forces. We could use the term here that is usually used in spiritual science: the formative forces of the life-body.

What do we mean here by life processes? This time we can take man as our starting point. Think of a child being born. It takes its first breath, draws in air, and then continues to breathe for its whole life. Breathing is a life process. At birth it already has circulation and the ability to generate its own body warmth. The infant then receives milk, and digestion begins. Excretion also begins, and replacing shed skin and old blood cells, and the maintenance or self-reproduction of the body. The child begins to grow.

From a spiritual-scientific perspective, Steiner distinguishes seven life processes: respiration, warming, digestion, excretion, maintenance, growth, reproduction. These are all well-known life processes. Only maintenance is not usually regarded as a process in its own right. It concerns forces which, for example, ensure that the second teeth in man last for decades, that fruit will keep, or that seeds remain viable.

The forces of the seven life processes are different from the morphogenic forces mentioned earlier. What sort of forces are they? They are forces of ethericity, forces of the etheric or life-body. They are manifestations of life. The same applies to them as was quoted concerning the origin of morphogenic forces (see page 10): we must look for 'modifying effects from heavenly bodies outside the earth,' that combine the four etheric forces into unified action in the etheric body. So what is it that transforms the tendency of etheric forces to strive towards the periphery, destroying earthly substances, into a constructive living collaboration? Rudolf Steiner writes: 'This transition into formlessness is *modified* by influences from the sun and similar influences from cosmic space.'[20] We can try to understand this indication by asking: Who or what then is the origin of life as such on earth? And we would have to say: the sun. Without light and warmth from the sun there would be no life on earth. The sun is the source of life. Life is an effect of the etheric body. The sun must therefore draw together the four ethers in the universe into an archetypal etheric body which is the life of the whole cosmos, and from which all life on earth is derived.

The Planetary Source of Morphogenic forces

The universe is a totality, the greatest individual, the One and the All. And this All lives. Today this knowledge is not taken for granted. And yet the All, like every living organism, evinces the three fundamental facts: form, life, substance. The stars in their ordered constellations give the form, the earth its substantiality, but stars also have substance, and the whole is alive through the sun and its wandering planets. The seven planets are the life of the world. The cosmic All was once far more alive, and humanity sensed and was aware of this life. The All-life had to withdraw and knowledge of it disappear in order for man to attain a free self-consciousness. Consciousness is always developed at the cost of life-development, is always connected with a devolution of life.

Thus the sun generates the power that unites the four ethers into a life-body. Life from the sun is modified by forces exerted by the six planets. But, just as it shares its light with them, so the sun also shares its life. We could say that every planet is the source of a life process which however would not be possible without the sun. We can now understand why Rudolf Steiner puts a planetary symbol by each of the seven life processes.[21]

The Seven Life Processes[22]

♄	Breathing	Consumption	
♃	Warming	Combustion	Ahrimanic
♂	Digestion	Deposition	
☉	Secretion		
♀	Maintenance	Hardening	
☿	Growth	Maturation	Luciferic
☽	Reproduction	Generation	

Pairs of closer connections also arise here: warming—growth, digestion—maintenance, etc. The correlation with the planets comes from an indication by Steiner in *Das Rätsel des Menschen* [The Riddle of Man]. The difference (in sequence) between Venus and Mercury in life-processes and life-stages is connected with the question of the occult Mercury and occult Venus.[23]

The most important aspect here is secretion. It contains the sun's power of separation, of individualization. The sun individualizes by creating separate living organisms. Sun-ether is the force which, while it takes effect, keeps the plant apart from the earth's forces. Without it, for example at night, the plant succumbs to the earthly forces.

Rudolf Steiner indicated that the three upper and three lower planetary forces are subject to a further kind of modification which leads them as it were beyond a middle position [of balance]. The forces bringing this about are those which in anthroposophy are called luciferic (for the three lower planets) and ahrimanic (for the three upper planets). Through their influences they transform the life-processes into the effects set out in the table above. The sun remains free, maintains the centre and harmonizes these effects.

Both these normal and modified planetary influences are physiologically active in organisms. Physiology and biology will gain tremendous clarity and order when their highly complex subject matter is illuminated by a knowledge of this. In anthroposophical science and medicine this is also just at a beginning.

When we study the seven wandering stars, we find that they present themselves to earthly man in a threefold way: through their *light*, their *velocity*, and their *distance* from the earth. Each of these aspects results in an effect in organic life. Each generates a different kind of life activity: light, the seven life-processes; velocity, the seven inner motions; and distance, the seven life-stages.

The Seven Inner Motions[24]

♄ Motion of uprightness
♃ Motion of thought
♂ Motion of speech
☉ Motion of the blood
☿ Motion of the glands
♀ Motion of respiration
☽ Motion of reproduction

According to Rudolf Steiner there are seven inner motions—and only seven.[25] The motion of uprightness is the one at work primarily in learning to stand and walk.

The Seven Life Stages[26]

	Life of:	
♄	Sensation (the senses)	Dying life
♃	Nerves	Preserving life (*Bewahrendes Leben*)
♂	Respiration	Form-giving life (*Bildendes Leben*)
☉	Circulation	the Changing image-forms of organs (*Sich verändernde Organbilder*)
☿	Movement	Energizing life (*Kraftendes Leben*)
♀	Metabolism	Material organs
☽	Reproduction	Self-renewing life

The seven life stages give the total life of the human being a sevenfold structure from above downwards. Life in the senses, the nerves, has a quality distinct from that in metabolism. Rudolf Steiner characterizes the almost spatially anatomical differentiations in the right-hand column of the above table as a more inward activity.[27] They are comprehensible through physiological factors.

Each sense organ is virtually a physical apparatus (e.g. the eye) in which life is strongly subservient to physical laws. Nerve-life preserves memory. Air is not just a chemically definable gas but is permeated with formative forces radiating into it from the periphery. With every breath of respiration the human being takes in these formative forces which pass from the lungs into the blood, and are carried by the blood into the whole organism. These blueprints of the organs are filled with substance in the metabolic life.

We need to bear in mind that these three-times-seven life-activities are all present in the life-body at the same time and inter-permeate each other. They give rise to life in the human being.

When we imagine the same in the cosmos, where the seven planets are in a constant state of change—constantly changing the intensity of their light, their distance and velocity—we get an inkling of the richness and multiplicity of cosmic life. This abundance is unimaginable. And yet we participate in it when, at the beginning of our embryonic phase, we structure and individualize our etheric body. The life-*activities* are connected primarily with the planetary *spheres*. The human being bears the planets as *heavenly bodies* in himself as life-*centres* in his seven planetary organs: heart—Sun; lung—Mercury; liver—Jupiter; gall—Mars; kidneys—Venus; spleen—Saturn; brain and sexual organs—Moon.[28]

These life-activities, in appropriately adapted form, are also present in animal and plant.

It will require astronomers, embryologists, musicians and physiologists to work together in order to unlock the connection of the physiology of the life-body's organs with the cosmos. In anthroposophical literature there are already some individual results of research in this area.

Rhythm

There is a principle in the realm of the planets and life-activities without which the world and man could not exist: rhythm. Day and night alternate rhythmically, as do the seasons. Rhythm is in respiration and circulation which in their rhythmic relationship form the foundation of all organic rhythmicity. Science has discovered an almost boundless number of rhythms in living organisms: rhythm in body temperature, rhythm in blood sugar and other substances in the blood, rhythm in bile constituents, rhythm in cell division, rhythms of growth, etc.

But what is rhythm? From a *practical* perspective everyone knows what rhythm is. Rhythm is practised everywhere, in music, in dance, education, medicine, agriculture, etc. In science there are a number of definitions, but no single view. The most common definition says 'rhythm is the repetition of similar events in similar time intervals'. Ludwig Klages published an important work in 1933 on the nature of rhythm in which he describes rhythm as polarized continuity (*polarisierte Stetigkeit*).[29]

Roda Wieser examined the fundamental concepts of polarity and periodicity in her work *Rhythmus und Polarität in der Handschrift* [Rhythm and polarity in handwriting].[30] Gunther

Hildebrandt thanks modern medicine and physiology for the far-reaching knowledge of rhythm in the human organism.[31]

But there is still no adequate understanding of rhythm. Rhythm is something that occurs in time and is connected with movement. A water wave, or indeed a sine wave, is often presented as an image of rhythm. It is neither of these, for they are both constant and rhythm is discontinuous.

Does a sequence of bell chimes or other sounds give us a rhythm? Again, no—they are uniform sequences. In rhythm there is irregularity, opposition: high—low, short—long, etc.

We can consider something we all know or can observe. When we hear a uniform series of strokes, e.g. a bell or metronome, after a while we begin to differentiate the stokes and group them, usually into groups of two. Ding—dong, ding—dong, loud—soft, loud—soft. Then we can reverse the accentuation and listen differently: dong—ding, dong—ding, soft—loud, soft—loud. When we do this, we feel we need to engage our will inwardly to make the reversal.

Now we can take a sequence of opposites, short—long, short—long, short—long, or something similar. Is this rhythm? That depends on whether we look at the group quantitatively or qualitatively, at its sequentiality or its opposites. If I say the 'short' is first and the 'long' is second, then I am just counting—one, two. The sequence, the 'one-following-the-other' is important. This is beat. One, two, three, one, two, three—a quantitative perspective. The quantitative quality is also evident in the fact that in a 2/4 beat, each quarter can be substituted by two eighths—it is just a question of having the complete quantity.

We find something different when we look at the opposites: short—long, loud—soft. These opposites are not arbitrary; inwardly they belong to one another. Long and soft can occur together, but they are not real opposites. One and two are also not opposites. Loud and soft, high and low are opposites belonging to each other within an overarching unity of quality, e.g. of volume or pitch.

We could also say that one and two are indifferent to each other. Real opposites are not indifferent; indeed, we could almost say they invoke one another. And this especially because they follow each other in movement, in time. If I count 'one . . .' which is to be followed by 'two', then what follows is something that is a number, a quantity, which at most has a place value, namely that of being second. But when a 'short', as a component of opposites, has faded away, then there is something invisible, inaudible, imperceptible present that anticipates the opposite. The sound that has faded away is as though transformed into its opposite. It is the separating and binding quality of the higher unity of opposites that is present. We could also formulate it like this: 'the first component of the opposites has faded and passed away, but has left behind an expectation that the second component will come'.

There is actually a threefoldness here: something that has faded away, the expectation, and something that is still to come. Past, present and future. Now we no longer have beat, but rhythm. Rhythm is something threefold, trinitarian. Loud—soft, high—low are not only opposites, but within their movement as rhythm they are polarities with something in between. But what is the nature of this middle element in rhythm? It is something that cannot be perceived and yet is active in the sense world. Rudolf Steiner calls rhythm something that is half spiritual. Here this becomes clear. The middle element—the connecting element uniting and separating the polarities—is like the power of the present, the 'now' between past and future.

There is something deeply mysterious in 'now'. There is only one actual 'now', which is the same for all human beings, uniting them in time. This power also lives in rhythm. Therefore whatever has the same rhythm is united and joined. This occurs not by compulsion but in freedom.

A single beat or single foot of verse is not yet beat or rhythm. They must first appear in a whole sequence. And then another relationship to time becomes evident.

We can take a series of iambs [the short-long or unstressed-stressed rhythm in poetry], for example in the poem by Conrad Ferdinand Meyer: *'Bemeßt den Schritt! Bemeßt den Schwung! Die Erde bleibt noch lange jung.'** No two iambs are the same. Or we can take the Danube waltzes of Johann Strauss. The beat in waltz-time is always the same, is repetition. But each beat carries the melody forward and is different. So: *beat repeats, rhythm transforms.*

But how does this relate to the rhythms in man, in organisms? Let's take the biorhythm of body temperature, for example. It is low in the first hours after midnight and at its highest in the afternoon. Blood sugar also undergoes rhythmic variations. The pulse too is a rhythm of this nature.

What are we measuring in these rhythms? The temperature level, the sugar content, the number of pulse beats. We are measuring quantities. A great many of the physiological rhythms in man and living organisms are *quantitative* rhythms.

But then there are other rhythms. The typical one is the rhythm of waking and sleeping. In essence this cannot be measured. Waking—sleeping, conscious—unconscious alternate. Something different is happening here. In this rhythm human beings grow older. Time is not there just to count pulse beats in temporal units. Time is itself active in this rhythm and changes people. Due to time, through waking and sleeping, a person is different on Tuesday from what they were on Monday, they have a different quality. It is a *qualitative* rhythm. This rhythm doesn't just repeat itself, it transforms.

The highest level of rhythm is reached when rhythm is harmonized with rhythm, when a rhythmic relationship is created such as in the breath and pulse, one to four. One could call it a *pure* rhythm. The physical element of the polarities vanishes in it. 'The physical as a thing vanishes in rhythmic processes.'[32]

---

*For English readers we can take a poem by Tennyson that has the same rhythm: 'On either side the river lie / Long fields of barley and of rye..'.

The ratio of one to four is actually a fundamental factor of human existence, not just in the relation of breath to pulse but also of man to the four elements, to the four stages of evolution, the four seasons, etc. In breath and pulse it is the relationship of two rhythms.

What then is the middle element holding breath-rhythm and pulse-rhythm together? The 'I' or Ego. The Ego is something spiritual that is present or active in the 'to' of one *to* four. It is the power of the centre. This force also creates a centre in the human form, giving rise to the threefoldness of the human body, the division into above, middle, and below. The human body is trinitarian, as seen in nerve-sense system, rhythmic system, and metabolic-limb system. Steiner presented his findings in this area in great detail, thereby giving humanity a foundation of knowledge that can be fruitful in all areas of life—in education, medicine, social life, and the understanding of nature, to name a few. Half a century of experience in all these areas has confirmed their enlivening effect.

Now let us look more closely at the human *rhythmic system*. At its heart is the relation of breath to pulse. Two other rhythms accompany these, one orientated upwards, the other downwards: the rhythm of waking and sleeping, and the rhythm of digestion. Steiner indicated that the rhythmic system encompasses all these four rhythms, and the power uniting them, the centre of the centre, is the Ego. This is why the rhythmic system, the working together of these four, is completely individual, and a doctor is able to read a great deal about the health or illness of a person from their relationship. There is nothing fixed or permanent in this system; it is immensely adaptable and variable, and is virtually inexhaustible and tireless. For decades, an entire lifetime, it is able to overcome stresses, disturbances and constraints, and to maintain its rhythmic interplay. The rhythmic system is the bearer and source of health. There is an occult rule that says 'rhythm substitutes energy' (*Rhythmus ersetzt Kraft*).

When we look at these four rhythms of the rhythmic system

we find new and wonderful interrelationships. The existence of quantitative and qualitative rhythms was discussed above. The pulse is a quantitative rhythm, the waking-sleeping rhythm is qualitative. It is not difficult to grasp that the rhythm of food belongs on the quantitative side. In people it is usually the least rhythmic, with eating times and food quantities being arbitrary. Here the function of the spleen plays a mediating role in conforming the non-rhythmic intake of food to the rhythmic system. While Steiner was still alive, and at his request, Lili Kolisko did research into this area and discovered this rhythmicizing function of the spleen.[33] Respiration belongs to the upper rhythms and is qualitative. With every breath we absorb formative forces and are subtly transformed by them.

The rhythmic system thus consists of two upper, qualitative, changing rhythms, and two lower, quantitative, repetitive ones, held together by the Ego. The rhythmic system, as the archetype of rhythm, is itself change and repetition.

Every rhythm is basically comprised of both change and repetition. In the course of time, qualitative rhythms also repeat, and quantitative rhythms change. So rhythm can be defined as the relationship of change to repetition. If we write this trinitarian fact, 'change—to—repetition', and imagine that each part could stand independently on its own, then pure change becomes melody, pure repetition becomes beat, and what connects them becomes harmony. We need to remember that we are talking about rhythm here. If we wished to characterize music, we could say it consists of melody, harmony and rhythm.

With this understanding of rhythm as change in repetition, we have grasped an archetypal principle, the primordial fact of life. All life occurs through change and repetition. Repetition is the principle of the etheric body, change is that of the astral body. They relate to each other like water and air, like pulse and breath.

Rhythm is a principle that reigns throughout creation. From where does it enter creation? What is its origin? The sun! All rhythms on earth come from the sun, even the cosmic ones. The sun is the source of rhythm just as it is the source of life. This is why life and rhythm are so closely tied together.

This can be shown symbolically. The sun combines the cruciform fourfold periphery into the archetypal etheric body in which rhythm operates—depicted in Diagram 17 as a lemniscate. This is also the symbol of a living organism.

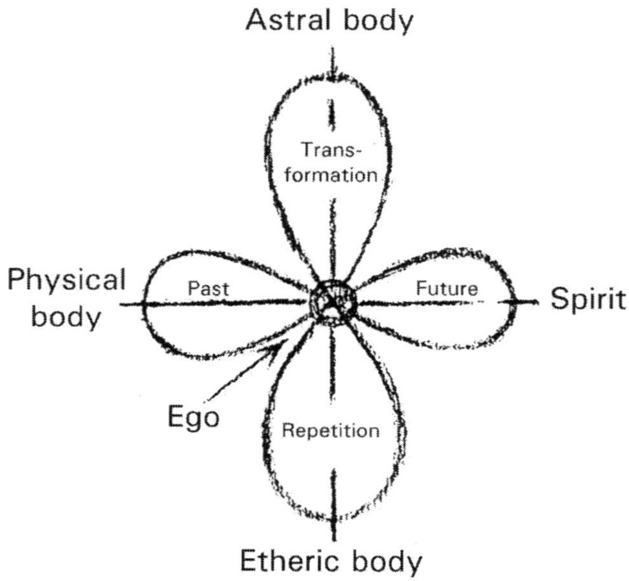

Diagram 17: Symbol of Rhythmicity

That the sun is the source of all rhythms becomes evident when we look at the principal rhythms in the human being and their numerical relationships. A person breathes on average 18 times per minute, so 60 times 18 times 24 equals 25,920 times per day. A full human life lasts around 72 years—72 times 360 equals 25,920 days. The position of the sun at the spring equinox moves through the whole zodiac in a Platonic year consisting of 25,920 years. Steiner never tired of drawing people's attention to these relationships.[34]

Thus the human being is the bearer of cosmic rhythms, which can be demonstrated in a variety of ways. Other rhythms are connected not directly with the sun but with a planetary rhythm.

This means that although the human being bears cosmic rhythms, these rhythms are not synchronized with the cosmos. The plant still lives in close connection with the cosmos; in its evolutionary ascent the animal emancipates itself from the cosmos more and more. Man has separated off his rhythms from the cosmos. He has thereby become an independent being bearing the potential for freedom.

It will be the task of a broadened natural science increasingly to research the rhythms and organic processes of organisms in connection with the life of the cosmos.

Formative Forces of Substance

Substance—Matter—Processes

Recognizing and presenting the operation of ethericity in the realm of substance is extremely difficult but will also lead to essential insights.

When we look at a lily-of-the-valley, a hen, or a person, we recognize them by their appearance, by their shape and form, in short, by their exterior. This exterior appearance is the result of the life in these three organisms. The life processes and formative forces that operate there were discussed earlier. This exterior aspect limits and encloses an interior that is behind or under it. What is covered by the form is its *substance*. 'Substance' literally means, 'that which stands beneath'. This concrete meaning is the concept of *substance* used here: that which is under the form in question, which materially fills out the form and carries it. Form cannot exist without a medium. Substance is its medium.

Form and substance are concepts which since ancient times have not always been understood in the same way. Here, where we are dealing with the manifestation of the etheric, we use them to signify the outer appearance and the material interior of the organism.

It goes without saying that form and substance both arise in the individual life processes of plant, animal and man. Just as form is individual, so is substance. We should not let ourselves be distracted by present ideas of chemistry that immediately come to the fore, that everything consists of hydrogen, oxygen, chemical elements. This is not what is meant here. Here we mean the fact that lily-of-the-valley substance can only be found in lillies-of-the-valley, and hen substance only in hens. In human beings it is even the case that every individual has their own substance, different from anyone else's. That everyone has their own protein is the great problem in organ transplants.

In the organic world, form and substance arise together and cannot be separated. In the inorganic world they can be separated. The same coin form can be imprinted in silver, gold or chocolate. It is this inseparability of form and substance in living organisms that led, in its early days, to the division of modern chemistry into its organic and inorganic branches. It was considered that certain substances could only be produced by living processes in a living organism. Then in 1827 Friedrich Wöhler synthesized organic matter for the first time—an event that had far-reaching consequences. Today chemistry is able to synthesize most of the substances occurring in organisms; it has even learnt to produce entirely new substances—synthetics—that exist neither in organic nor inorganic nature.

We will now consider something which we have hitherto only touched on. When we think about our description of formative forces and life processes, it becomes clear that these are general forces. What has been described is the forming of a leaf *in general*, not a specific rose leaf or linden leaf, not the circulation in the nettle, a trout, or man. These general formative forces require the addition of a specific 'species-forming' agency. Only then does a structure arise that exists in nature. Only specific plants and animals exist in sense-perceptible nature. In the human kingdom each individual has the quality of a species, is their own kind. Even in the inorganic world there is never just matter, but always specific matter, substances. That is the difference between substance and matter.

In the inorganic realm substance is also always indicative of matter with specific attributes and qualities making it unique. Copper, arsenic, nitrogen are all species of matter just as the lily-of-the-valley and the violet are specific species of plant. The substances of the inorganic realm are the chemical elements.

So what is *matter*? This is the term for 'stuff' without qualities, materiality *per se*. It has to have at least one attribute however, otherwise it could not be a part of the sense world. This attribute is occupation of space, 'spaciality'. Matter is the space-filling element, as described in Volume I. But this characteristic does not signify more than, for example, the white colour of the lily-of-the-valley or the weight of a hen. By no means does matter mean something existing in itself, something immutable. We can say that matter, the occupying of space, is just one attribute of all substances, but not their foundation. There is no matter *per se* as something existing in itself.

The theory (= view) of present science that matter is the fundamental substance of the sensory world is based on its materialistic worldview. It is the consequence of an error in thinking, of observation that does not take all the phenomena into account.

In Volume I we distinguished between positive space (brought about by physical forces) and negative space (brought about by the four etheric forces). It would therefore make sense to distinguish between *positive and negative matter*. In the sense world every substance has the attribute of positive matter, that is, it fills a position in space. A substance would be negatively material if it filled negative space or etheric space. So we need to ask: Is there a corresponding situation for matter, for substance, whereby it rises into the region of the ethers, the periphery? Yes, indeed! All matter is itself condensed from the starry heights and can ascend to them again. Then it becomes process. The metallic gold in front of me is gold process come to rest. Gold process fills the cosmos up to the vault of the heavens. But the liver too, as a physical organ, is liver process come to rest. Liver process permeates the whole organism, indeed the whole cosmos. *Thus every substance needs to be recognized as process come to rest.* In nature, matter and form always occur united. Just as in the physical realm every form is movement come to rest, so every kind of matter is process come to rest.[35]

We can therefore write:

etheric:	Movement	+	Process
	↓		↓
physical:	Form	+	Matter

In this way we grasp a true totality. What combines the fourfoldness into a particular unity is that which, in the true categorical sense, can be called substance, e.g. gold, arnica.

The Three Zodiacal Crosses of Substance

This brings us back to the question: What are these higher-level forces that configure general formative forces into a specific form, giving rise to the unique characteristics of a species? The specific species is the effect, the expression, the 'manifestation-form' of a being.

Diagram 18, as a reflection of mediaeval thinking, shows a woodcut in which a man, leaving the sensory world, penetrates the periphery of the heavens and perceives behind it the prevailing archetypal images and beings portrayed in symbolic forms. The man, by means not of sensory forces but of supersensory ones, penetrates the periphery of heaven and perceives spiritual beings. These are spaceless and timeless, or put symbolically, they are on the other side of the boundary of heaven that encompasses the spacial-temporal world. The beings of 'kinds', the archetypes of species, exist in that spiritual world. It is the world of the spiritual hierarchies which, in their totality, we can call the *Cosmic Word* or Logos.

Diagram 18: Wanderer at the edge of the world

If we compare this picture with our diagram on page 14 [Diagram 2] of the horizon and formative forces, it becomes clear that it is these archetypes, the beings of the species, that draw together the formative forces in a particular way, thus determining a specific organism. We presented the stars, the zodiac, and the planets as the origin of formative forces and life functions.

The same stars, when in darkness *below* the horizon, act as substance-building forces; there they shape as interior that which fills out with matter and bears the form's outer expression. Starlight shines in the darkness and condenses to materiality. So to be accurate, both the working of the species-beings' forces and the stellar formative forces should also be placed below the horizon. Then the relationship of the substance half [of the diagram] to the higher worlds becomes clear. Then we can see how substance-building stellar forces always operate *through* the earth from below, are active below the surface, generating matter as it were through the central point of the earth. We cannot show this visibly because it takes place in the dark interior. But we can think it and present the interrelationships in the form of thoughts.

These interrelationships have already been researched in detail and presented by Rudolf Hauschka in his *Substanzlehre* [Study of substance].[36] From his phenomenological investigations, Hauschka distinguished three times four substance processes that are the basis of all organic development. Also evident for him was the connection of these substances with the zodiac, emerging as three 'cosmic crosses': the atmospheric, oceanic and mineral crosses. Hauschka described the full cross of the zodiacal constellations as the primordial homes of processes which, when completed and fixed on earth, result in the well-known substances of the earth (see Diagram 19).

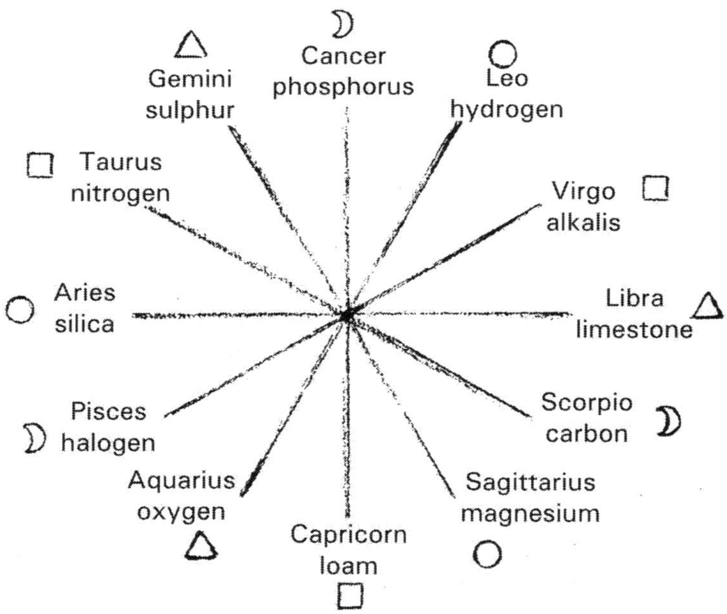

Diagram 19: Substance-building forces of the zodiac

Whereas in the zodiacal trigons the formative forces all belong to the same classical element, here, in the crosses of substance-building constellations, all four classical elements work together.

The detailed connections are as follows:

Atmospheric cross	Oceanic cross	Mineral cross
○ Leo – hydrogen	Δ Gemini – sulphur	☽ Cancer – phosphorus
□ Taurus – nitrogen	☽ Pisces – halogen	○ Aries – silica
Δ Aquarius – oxygen	○ Sagittarius – magnesium	□ Capricorn-clay/loam
☽ Scorpio – carbon	□ Virgo – alkalis	Δ Libra – limestone

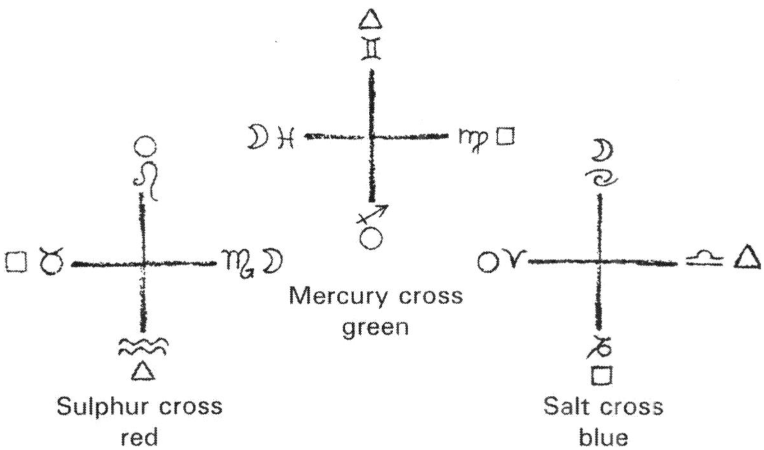

Diagram 20: The three substance crosses according to Hauschka

The cosmic cross of Leo, Aquarius, Taurus and Scorpio – four constellations that have always held a place of prominence in the zodiac – can also be called the astral or sulphur cross. Their collaboration produces *protein substance,* the basis of life for all independent organisms. The plant also forms protein in the area concerned with the preservation of the species, namely the seed.

The cross comprising Cancer, Capricorn, Aries and Libra – called the physical or salt cross – brings together substance-building processes which ultimately produce the entire *solid mineral earth.* Just as silica and limestone processes have produced the mountain formations of the earth from living plant and animal organisms that have hardened into mineral, so also the phosphoric and sculptural loam processes are connected with blood and nerve in man and lead to ossification and sclerosis processes. Precisely in the formative forces of this cosmic cross we see how everything that is dead [i.e. mineral] in nature has arisen from macrocosmic life-processes.

The collaboration in the cross comprising Gemini, Sagittarius, Pisces and Virgo—also called the etheric or Mercury cross—gives rise to the *soluble salts of the oceans*. Its substance processes are seen in every living organism as functions of dissolving and binding, mediating and healing. The water of the oceans, which has incalculable amounts of sulphuric-acidic magnesium and cooking salt dissolved in it, is also the origin of all life on earth.

All twelve substance-building processes always act together in *every* organism. They are drawn together by the being of each species in a species-specific way, or were drawn together at the beginning of its development. Substance-formational processes are organized in every substance according to the three principles above, and are present in differing combinations in every substance in nature. In medieval alchemy and pharmacology, knowledge of the three principles of salt, mercury and sulphur (*principium* = beginning) was the basis for their understanding of medicinal remedies.

This knowledge has been completely lost and needs today to be attained anew. The dominant analytical chemistry and pharmacology of the present has barely noticed that anthroposophical pharmacology is based on a significantly different view of substance founded on the therapeutic relationship between the human being and these three principles in nature. The three principles—salt, mercury and sulphur—are combined in various and specific ways in every substance.[37]

The Planets and the Formative Forces of Substance in Metals

Substance-forming forces do not only emanate from the zodiac; they also come from the planets. Steiner specified how the seven primary metals are connected with the planets, which has been substantiated in experiments by many anthroposophical researchers.[38]

Thus lead belongs to Saturn, tin to Jupiter, iron to Mars, gold to the Sun, copper to Venus, quicksilver to Mercury, and silver to the Moon.

Other metals arose by several planetary influences working together, for example, antimony from the planets below the sun—Moon, Mercury and Venus.

Hauschka's investigations were focussed on exploring the working together of zodiacal formative impulses with those of the planetary spheres. Using the image of the spiral of creation, he attempted to connect the cosmic genesis of substances with the order of the periodic table.

The aphoristic remarks above have already been verified in an anthroposophically broadened approach in chemistry, pharmacology, botany and medicine, where they have proved fruitful and are constantly being investigated and developed further. We refer the reader here to the original scientific literature.

5. The Nature of Potentizing

Potentizing and potentized remedies are a strange thing. Potentized remedies have existed for more than 150 years, and during this long period countless doctors and laymen worldwide have used them, tested and experienced their healing efficacy. Official science and medicine however are unfamiliar with these remedies and have no relationship to them; they reject them or view them as fantasy. This entirely negative evaluation is a disquieting problem. The healing power and efficacy of potentized remedies is beyond doubt. It is simply not the case that for a century and a half generations of doctors, as homoeopaths and trained and experienced observers, have been deluding themselves and deceiving others. And when, like the author, one has run a general medical practice for 40 years using almost exclusively potentized remedies, one knows the efficacy of these remedies and uses high potencies with confidence and successful results.

So what is the cause of this discrepancy of views? The question leads to the fundamental problem of science, namely, that when a fact arises or is experienced, it must also be conceptually understood. Experience on its own may suffice for action, but not for understanding. Hahnemann's teaching is based on the most exact observations and experience. He is a pure empiricist, keeping to the phenomena and avoiding any kind of theorizing. He gathered an immense wealth of experience in potentization and potentized remedies, but could not penetrate this wealth intellectually (in the form of ideas). He could act out of experience, and this has remained the situation in the use of these remedies from Hahnemann's time to the present. Official medicine and science, lacking both the experience and the familiarity with these remedies that comes through using them, are baffled by them. An uncomprehended fact—for example, a potentized remedy—is intellectually disquieting. Only when the relationship of that fact to other facts and knowledge is established, does the disquiet settle. Percept (experience) and concept together give us knowledge. In a situation where this resolution has not been reached, we can relate to the uncomprehended fact in a number of ways: we can ignore it, take no note of it, or deny it and declare it to be nonsense and fantasy. Both have occurred again and again in the last 150 years with regard to potentization. From this the only conclusion we can draw is that potentization cannot be understood by means of the conceptual framework and ideas prevalent in medicine and natural science hitherto. This lack of understanding applies also to homoeopaths themselves; they too can offer no other insights. Just read in this regard the two articles, *Das Hochpotenzproblem* [The problem of high potencies] and *Im Dschungel der homöopathischen Potenzen* [In the jungle of homoeopathic potencies], in the *Allgemeinen Homöopatischen Zeitung* [General journal of homoeopathy] (founded in 1832!), edition 1/1971.[39]

So must we simply forgo a conceptual solution to the problem of high potencies? And what is the problem exactly? It is this: through a particular way of treating and preparing substances—namely by potentizing them—the same substances begin to show new and previously unknown effects when introduced into a living organism as remedies. These new properties in the substances cannot be explained by the ideas currently recognized in chemistry and physics. If we consider the present categories of chemistry and physics as the only possible ones for an understanding of matter, then these new, different effects remain inexplicable.

So what is needed here? A science which, to use Hahnemann's expression, also knew and understood the 'spirit-like' (*geistartig*) effects and properties of substance. This science already exists; it is the anthroposophical spiritual science created by Rudolf Steiner in the first quarter of the twentieth century. It has had a similar fate to homoeopathy: officially ignored or rejected yet having a strong effect. In a course given by Steiner in 1920 for doctors and medical students,[40] he formulated the insights necessary for an understanding of potentization. When we look at these ground-breaking indications, it becomes clear that potentization is a question of central importance for our knowledge of nature and the human being. It can only be grasped through an understanding of the essential relationship between substance and organism, by means of a new science of nature and man that takes the spiritual into account. It is a matter of answering questions such as: What actually happens during potentization? What is the nature of the new forces that appear? How are they related to nature and man? Why are they healing forces? What is their relationship to the human organism?

We will try to give some answers in the following.

It will be helpful here to quote again the basic indications given by Hahnemann. In the 1842 sixth edition of his *Organon of the Art of Healing*, he writes:

> § 269. The homopathic art of medicine develops for its use, to a hitherto unheard-of degree, the inner, spirit-like medicinal powers of raw substances by means of a process peculiar to homoeopathy and which in my time had never been tried, whereby all the substances become penetratingly, indeed immeasurably efficacious and remedial, *even those that in the raw state give no evidence of the slightest medicinal power on the human body.* This remarkable change in the properties of natural bodies develops the latent, hitherto unperceived, as if slumbering and hidden, *dynamic powers* which influence predominantly the life principle and the well-being of animal life. This is effected by mechanical action upon the smallest particles [of the substance] which, by means of grinding and shaking, *are separated from each other by a neutral substance, dry or fluid, interposing itself between them.* This process is called *dynamizing, potentizing* (development of medicinal power) and the products are dynamizations or potencies in different degrees.[41]

Hahnemann's footnote:

> We still hear daily how homoeopathic medicinal potencies are referred to as *mere* dilutions, when they are the very opposite; they are a true unlocking of the substances as they occur in nature, and bringing to light and revealing the hidden specific medicinal powers contained in their inner nature, which are brought forth by grinding and shaking. The aid of a chosen, non-medicinal medium of attenuation is but a *secondary condition.* Dilution alone—for example the solution of a grain of salt—is just water; the grain of salt will disappear in a dilution with a large quantity of water, and will never become the salt remedy which, by means of our carefully prepared dynamization, is raised to most marvellous power.

From footnote § 270:

> It is highly probable through this that the material, by means of such dynamization (development of its true, inner, curative essence), will ultimately dissolve completely into its individual spirit-like essence. In its crude state therefore it could be considered actually to consist only of this undeveloped spirit-like essence.

In his note to § 11, Hahnemann compares the dynamic medicinal effect with the effect of a magnet on a piece of iron. He then continues:

> It is not in the corporeal atoms of these highly dynamized remedies, nor their physical or mathematical surfaces (by which people still—and vainly—wish to regard the high energies of dynamized remedies as material) that the medicinal energy is found. But rather there is, invisibly in the moistened pillule or its solution, a specific medicinal force, exposed and released as far as possible from the medicinal substance, which by contact with living animal fibre works energetically (*dynamisch*) on the whole organism (but without communicating to it anything of a material nature, no matter how rarefied this is imagined to be). The freer and more immaterial it has become through dynamization, the greater the effect.[42]

For the modern reader, these statements, written by Hahnemann at the age of 86 at the end of an immensely full life, are initially difficult to understand because they are full of unfamiliar ideas and can give the impression of just being theory. But they are full of concisely formulated observations and experiences. We also sense, however, how difficult it is to understand and formulate these new facts. Hahnemann emphasizes strongly that these new forces are not atomic or material attributes of the substances, nor are we dealing with dilution in the usual sense. Had this been taken seriously, the innumerable attempts and arguments to justify or question the effectiveness or otherwise [of the remedies] down to the last molecule (Loschmidt's number) could have been omitted, and the problem of high potencies approached from a different angle. Hahnemann describes with great exactitude the releasing of forces through the procedure he simply terms 'potency' or 'dynamization' from the Latin and Greek. He doesn't posit a theory; he simply gives his findings a name. His term *'spirit-like'* (*geistartig*) is also not theory; it simply points to the differentness and non-material nature of the effect. For Hahnemann the life-processes in the organism are also spirit-like. The dynamizations and potentized substances work on this spirit-like dynamic life-force and its pathological changes.

The medical and scientific establishment did not accept Hahnemann's experience and view; indeed they could not, for the development of science was such that only the material aspect of the organism was taken into account. It required the emergence of a spiritual science that is able with reliable methods to investigate the spiritual component of man and nature, not only sense-perceptible phenomena. This broadened understanding of man and cosmos through spiritual scientific investigation was created by Rudolf Steiner in anthroposophy. This also made possible a broadening of medicine, which Steiner presented in a number of lectures and courses, and finally in his book co-authored with Ita Wegman, *Grundlegendes für eine Erweiterung der Heilkunst nach geisteswissenshaftlichen Erkenntnissen* [Foundation for a broadening of medicine according to spiritual-scientific knowledge].

So what was the impetus given by Steiner in 1920 that brought some progress into the question of potentization? As a first step we can summarize his indications under three aspects: the importance of how the remedies are prepared; the medium assumes a different configuration; potentization is a rhythmical process.

The technical procedure of preparing the potencies was described above: one part substance is mixed with nine parts medium (water, alcohol, lactose). One part of this is then mixed with nine parts of fresh medium, and so on. At each stage a potency is produced. This process can be repeated indefinitely, yet the process itself cannot determine how many times this should be.

What is the unique quality of this process? The production of a potency occurs in three phases. Firstly, a substance that is to be the content and essence of the potency is chosen and made ready. It will give the potency its substantial and individual characteristic. Then a ratio is determined between substance and medium, e.g. 1:10, 1:100, or some other ratio. Finally one part of the substance is combined with 9 or 99 parts of the medium and then mixed by succussion or trituration.

Producing a potency is therefore a process of three stages. Every stage determines something different. The first phase determines the potency according to substance and number in the sequence—it individualizes. The second phase establishes a relation, a ratio. The third is a thorough mixing by means of movement. These three phases of potency preparation relate to each other like the three systems of the threefold human organism: like the individualizing element of the head to the ratio-creating activity of the middle system (e.g. the ratio of one to four in breath and pulse), and to the mixing movement of the metabolic-limb system. This correspondence is a factor worthy of note.

These three processes are the foundation of every potency and make each into an individual unity. As each potency, following the first process described above, becomes the substance and foundation for a new one, and is then repeated, a series of potencies arises that is inwardly coherent. It is a type of generative sequence which is irreversible. One potency becomes the 'seed' for the next; it 'grows' through the medium and by means of succussion becomes a new unity. Potentization in a certain sense is a realm between the organic and the inorganic.

As one potency follows the other, as each arises from the other, they each acquire a number in the sequence. The initial substance is subjected to a numerical process; the lawfulness of whole numbers is imprinted into the substance.

Regarding the change in the effects of the substance, Hahnemann called this mode of preparation 'potentizing' or 'dynamizing'. If we want to give this mode of preparation, this method as such, a name that accords with its innate essence, we can call it 'steps' [or 'stages'] (*Stufen*) or 'staging' (*Stufung*). The step process is a way of handling substances, of acting upon them like melting or digesting, which causes new substance attributes to emerge. These then become evident in the medicinal use of the potencies or in biological experiments (plant experiments).

If we want to understand the changes caused by the steps, we must first take into account the effect of what we can call dilution. When producing decimal potencies, in the 6th potency there is only a millionth of the the original substance left, in the 12th potency a billionth, in the 25th or 30th there is, according to the present view of physics, not a single material particle left. Yet over and against this is the fact that even in these potencies the specific effect of the original substance is still present. In a potentizing sequence of 30 steps, experience shows that, if Arnica or quartz was the original substance, the specific Arnica or quartz effect is present at every stage. Every doctor who works with such remedies knows the characteristic effects of Arnica or quartz, and administers them accordingly in therapies of high potencies. The specificity of the original substance is consistently present even where mathematically there is no longer any of its matter left.

What does it mean to say there is no longer any [of the original] matter present? The prime characteristic of matter is mass, which we grasp (also mathematically) as weight. The fact that potency-effects persist beyond the limit calculable by Loschmidt's or Avogadro's number (around the 23rd potency), leads to the following insight.

There are two phases in the substance—a weighable, ponderable phase, and an unweighable, imponderable one. We can say: at the beginning, Arnica is in a weighable, ponderable condition; in high potencies it is in an unweighable, imponderable one. *Potentization is the conversion of a substance from a ponderable to an imponderable state.*

We are faced here with a hitherto unknown and unnoticed phenomenon. To understand it we need to look very closely at what happens when a substance is *diluted*. Clearly dilution is not a chemical action. So what is it? Substance is dispersed, separated out. Both Hahnemann and Steiner point to this crucial process: the 'smallest particles' of a substance 'are separated from each other by a neutral substance, dry or fluid, interposing itself between them' (Hahnemann); 'The aggregation, the coherence of the substance' is suspended (Steiner).

Present science does not pay coherence and its dissolution any particular attention. Yet this is the fundamental process in potentization which needs to be understood very exactly. The two sentences quoted above, by Hahnemann and Steiner, describe the process accurately and precisely, but they do not go into the forces involved. We need to look for these. Holding-together, coherence, aggregation is an effect of electromagnetic forces—of forces, in other words, that are connected with mass and can be calculated as potential. Overcoming them cannot be explained by purely mechanical forces. After all, mechanical forces are themselves also forces of mass. With trituration, that is by interposing a dry medium, there are clearly mechanical forces at work initially. In a dilution with water it becomes clear that not only mechanical forces but also forces of a different nature are at work.

To see this, we can look at the phenomenon of a salt crystal dissolving in water, e.g. a small crystal of potassium permanganate.

The crystal falls into the liquid and dissolves, i.e. its original form disappears. Then, after some time, all the liquid is uniformly coloured. Which forces are at work here? When we say, 'the water dissolves the salt,' this is not strictly accurate. The effect of water as a liquid medium is seen in the principle of buoyancy, Archimedes' principle. That is the actual effect of water, working by itself, in the case of an insoluble body. In the case of a soluble salt however, another force—a dividing, dispersing one—comes into play, which is not connected with buoyancy or weight, but is clearly independent of gravity. This can be seen in the fact that the salt is dispersed homogeneously throughout the liquid. 'Homogeneously' means the salt particles (molecules, ions) are distributed evenly, that is, there is an equal amount of them both at the top and the bottom of the container. This is only possible because gravity has been overcome. This dissolving, anti-gravity force takes hold of the salt substance not only with a dividing (quasi pulverizing) force, but also with an expanding, 'anti-centric' tendency.

We need here to picture a force that is the opposite of the concentrating [or contracting] force that leads to the holding-together or coherence of matter. Rudolf Steiner was the first to draw attention to the existence of these forces and to describe them. He called them 'universal' or 'etheric' forces in contrast to the central forces which are the ones known to physics and used in our technology.[43] Central forces (gravity, electricity, etc.) can all be described as deriving from a centre, and calculated and measured from a potential. The universal forces—whose origin mathematically speaking is in the periphery, in the infinitely distant plane just as the central forces' origin is in the gravitational centre—cannot be calculated or measured with the methods of measurement generally known today. This is indeed one of the reasons why these forces remain unknown to modern physics even though they manifest in many phenomena such as, for example, in the so-called negative geotropism of plants which, in the plant's tendency to grow towards the periphery, clearly shows an overcoming of gravity. These imponderable universal forces emerge in the 'steps' of potentization and make understandable the efficacy of high potencies which would otherwise be incomprehensible.

These forces emerging in the dissolving process of a salt crystal are also active in trituration. The equal status of dry or liquid stages can also be seen in the fact that the process can be transferred from a dry to a liquid medium, and that pillules sprinkled with potencies in liquid form will retain the potency. Indeed, one of Hahnemann's largely unacknowledged achievements was that he managed to take insoluble substances, like metallic gold or quartz, and render them soluble through trituration. It was facts like these that would meet with rejection or ridicule by future scientists, because they point to attributes of substance different from those considered possible from the modern materialist point of view.

A further consequence of the phenomena coming to light through potentization is the need to think of substance not only as matter in the sense of mass according to physics and the central forces, but equally determined by universal forces—indeed, it becomes necessary to view the whole of nature in this way, that is, to think of it as constituted by these two species of forces.

Steiner frequently stated the need for this new view. In the first lecture of his natural science course, he formulates it as follows:

> Where do we find a situation where only central forces are at work according to their potential, and where do we find one where universal forces are working which cannot be calculated as potentials? We can give an answer to this, but it immediately shows the essential point of view to which we must refer. We can say: In all the machines produced by man, which are put together from the elements of nature—this is where we find the purely abstract central forces according to their potentials. By contrast, what is out in nature—

> even inorganic nature—cannot be fully observed only according to central forces. That is not possible, it can't be done. Rather, the situation is that in all things that are not artificially produced by human beings there is a flowing together of both central and universal forces. In the entire realm of so-called nature we find nothing which, in the true sense, is not alive—except what man produces artificially, his mechanical devices, his machines.[44]

It is in a knowledge of central and universal forces, in the ponderable and imponderable factors, that the essential expanded foundation for an understanding of potentizing can be found. We can now look again at its three phases.

The first phase, as described above, needs no further explanation. It is the procedure that establishes the foundation, and as such is repeated, thereby entering into the sequential laws of number. The ratio of dilution, i.e. the measure of dilution, can be chosen at will—1:10, 1:100, or another ratio. Once chosen however, the same ratio must be maintained throughout the potentizing sequence. Research into the effect of potency sequences on plant growth, using a varying number of steps, resulted in similar graphs, with only different height levels. This is significant, indicating that it is not the mathematically calculable dilution that is crucial but the number of stages, the 'steps'. A C15 (centesimal) potency is therefore comparable to a D15 (decimal). From his investigations, Wilhelm Pelikan showed that a ratio of 1:10 is the most efficacious. This is connected with the secret of 'ten-ness', 1 + 9. Hahnemann used a C-potency almost exclusively, probably for practical reasons since a dilution of 1:100 is more easily managed.

The third stage of potentization—succussion or trituration—serves the relation of mix between substance and medium. In answer to a question from Lili Kolisko, Steiner indicated that it was a matter here of homogenizing the two components. Clearly it is not just a matter of mixing, but of bringing into operation the universal forces that work in the homogeneity. In the homogenizing process there is an optimal level. Kolisko designed a method of experimentation for determining this optimum.[45] The optimum succussion differs depending on the substance—for plant substances it is between two and two and a half minutes; for mineral substances it is around four minutes.

It is not possible to increase a potency beyond its optimum. This is important since the remedial effect of the beneficial qualities and character of the original substance depends on reaching this optimum.

If, as described above, potentization is the conversion of a substance from a ponderable to an imponderable state—in other words, the ponderable substance is 'got out of the way'—then the question arises: How is this possible, and how can the imponderable substance be retained and managed? Hahnemann recognized clearly the immaterial, imponderable, purely dynamic nature of the medicinal effect of high potencies, and also answered this question:

> By means of this mechanical operation, provided it is carried out properly according to the above instructions, a change is effected in the given substance, which in its crude state shows itself only as matter—at times even as non-medicinal matter—but by means of such higher and higher dynamization is changed and finally subtlized into spirit-like medicinal power which indeed *in itself* is not accessible to our senses but for which the medicinally prepared dried pillule, or even better when dissolved in water, becomes *the carrier,* and in this condition manifests the healing power of this invisible force in the sick body.[46]

Rudolf Steiner adds the following piece of knowledge to Hahnemann's view of the medium as the carrier of the effect: 'The medium attains a different configuration through the preparation.' At the beginning the substance shows the attributes of its ponderable state. By diluting, potentizing, more and more, Steiner says,

> I finally reach a zero-point at which the effects of this substance in its ponderable state no longer manifest. If I continue, however, it is not

> the case that the whole affair simply disappears, but rather that the opposite element emerges and that this opposite element is then worked into the surrounding medium. [...] just as I become a different person in outer social life if I go from wealth to indebtedness, so the substance converts to its opposite condition and then lends this opposite condition, which it had previously held within itself, to its environment.[47]

The medium has attained a different configuration. From a material, ponderable perspective there is nothing left, and yet the specific quality of the mother substance is present in the medium. Only the very latest physics has developed concepts that make such an immaterial effect thinkable. Using its terminology we could say: the medium has become the carrier of the Arnica information.[48] This is a concept that is possible in present physics. How it may be understood from a spiritual-scientific perspective will be discussed later.

Substance is converted by potentization into its opposite condition, which is now connected with the configuration of the medium. However, this conversion does not take place in a linear way. Seen externally, each potency follows the other in a uniform sequence. But a potentization sequence of, say, 30 potencies, conceals three hidden conditions through which the substance is taken.

> In the potentizing process we eventually come to a zero point. Beyond this point there are counter-effects. But that is not all: if we carry on beyond this zero point we can come to another zero point which in turn is a zero point for these counter-effects. Then, going beyond even this point, we can reach still higher effects, which indeed in their tendency come to the fore once again, but are constituted completely differently.[49]

Now we need to ask: what is a 'counter-effect', or 'opposite conditions'? We can take quartz or Arnica as our mother substance. They each have certain attributes. So what are their opposite attributes? At first, in potencies of D6, D15, D30, we do not have anything opposite, we still have Arnica or quartz effects. So what is this 'oppositeness' related to? It must be a general quality belonging to all substances, since the conversion applies to all mother substances. Rudolf Steiner indicates what the opposite effect is.

In the first section of the potentizing path—the two zero points divide it into three parts—it is 'aggregation, the coherence of the substance', its holding-together. This is made to vanish. So what now is the opposite of holding-together? Radiating, raying out. The substance then attains, according to Steiner, 'the property of radiating its former qualities into the surroundings.'[50] Thus, in the second part of the potentizing sequence, the substance has a radiating quality. And what, in the third part, is the opposite of raying out? Something that is again similar to holding-together, a conservation, a configuration. 'The medium attains a different configuration.' From this the complete contrast of the first and third parts becomes clear. There is a configuration in both of them: a configuration determined by the coherence of the substance, and the configuration of the medium. So what is the nature of the oppositeness? In its coherent configuration, the substance is ponderable; in the second configuration the substance has lost its weight, it has become imponderable. The middle part plays a transitional role from the first to the third part. It creates a balance between the ponderable and imponderable elements. It has no structure of its own, it is transitional, mobile, mercurial. It is the realm of interplay between substance and medium. After the first zero point, the substance begins 'to radiate into its surroundings, and in the appropriate way to stimulate the medium with which I process it.'[51] This happens during the whole of the middle part. In the end the substance has vanished, has gone completely into the medium. The medium has become a carrier for the imponderable.

The different behaviour of substance in the different parts of the potentizing process cannot be ascertained by analysing the potencies themselves, but by their effects on the living organism. At the end of the indication quoted above, Steiner mentioned that it would be a fine task to portray in certain graph forms the effects that emerge from potentizing. He described in principle how such a graph would look, being divided by two zero points and comprising three different areas of effect—the lower, middle and higher potencies. It would look schematically like this:

Diagram 21: Graph of potentization effects

Steiner's suggestion was taken up. Already in 1923 Lili Kolisko published her work, *Physiologischer und physikalischer Nachweis der Wirksamkeit kleinster Entitäten* [Physiological and physical evidence for the influence of the smallest entities]. From another of Steiner's indications, and following his advice, Frau Kolisko designed a method of plant research for demonstrating the effects of potencies on germinating wheat.[52] These experiments, which Kolisko herself continued for decades, became the starting point for extensive experimental research by a large number of scientists over almost half a century. The results have confirmed Steiner's indications. This is significant, for what Steiner investigated spiritual-scientifically has been confirmed by experimentation. Through the work of Kolisko and other researchers, the problem of proving the effects of potentized substances on people and on the course of illnesses has been resolved. It has been demonstrated using replicable methods with objects against which accusations of psychological or other delusions cannot be raised. This means that, after 150 years of homoeopathic experience, fructified by Steiner's ideas, and demonstrated by the experimental work of his students, potentization as a technical method of 'stepping', with its biological effects, is a fully ascertained fact. It needs now to be incorporated into the body of science, or science broadened so as to be able to understand it.

Graphs from the experiments show the two zero points predicted by Steiner, through which three zones of effects emerge, corresponding to what was presented theoretically above as the ponderable, middle and imponderable zones.

The polarity of effects in the first and third zones is not apparent in the plant growth experiments. More exact and subtle differentiation in growth is required here. But they are very visible and convincing in the crystallization experiments carried out by Alla Selawry, where contrary form tendencies arise in low and high potencies.[53]

The graphs also indicate what Steiner calls a rhythmical process. In the 1920 course he says: 'In nature everything is fundamentally based on rhythmical processes.'[54] He is pointing here to some unknown phenomenon which is hard to grasp with current scientific thinking. However, the experimental confirmation of his other indications can incline us to look also at this unusual perspective.

> When we consider the attributes of any substance, the attributes active in the substance as we find it, we initially have something which, when overcome by the organism during digestion, is absorbed into the lower human functions. But we can also 'homoeopathize' it, if I may put it like that. We can cancel out the substance's aggregation, its coherence. This happens when substance is diluted in some way, when, as just mentioned, one makes homoeopathic dosages. Something comes to light here which is not given proper notice in our current science, and people are so inclined to look at everything abstractly. Thus, when they have a light source, they say that the light radiates out on all sides, and they picture it spreading out on all sides—they picture this also for the sun—and then disappearing at infinity. But this is not the case. An activity of

> this nature never disappears at infinity but travels only to a limited sphere and then like elastic returns, even though its quality, its attributes, are then often different from the attributes it had on the outward journey [. . .]. In nature there are only rhythmical processes; there are no processes that run on to infinity, there is only that which returns rhythmically into itself.
>
> This is not only the case with quantitative raying out, but also with qualitative raying out. If you start to split up a substance, at the outset it has certain attributes. These attributes do not go on reducing infinitely, but, when a certain point is reached, they go into reverse and become the opposite attributes.[55]

Steiner takes up this theme again in a later lecture of the same course. He describes how, during the potentizing process, the ponderable attributes of the substance arrive at a zero point where they cease to behave as ponderable qualities, and how their opposite then emerges which is worked into the medium. The rhythmical process of potentizing can thus be described as the gradual alteration of a substance's attributes by bringing them to a zero point, after which other qualities emerge. Succussion and trituration are not rhythmical in this sense. The expression 'rhythmic dilution', meaning the ascent from stage to stage, is also not an accurate term, in the same way that the progression of whole numbers cannot be described as rhythmical.

From this we become aware that apart from rhythmic processes *(Prozessen)* there are also rhythmic events (*Vorgänge*), usual rhythms. What Steiner calls rhythmic processes are unknown in present-day science. The outward journey of an activity or quality only to a limited sphere and its rhythmical return into itself is not known today. What we generally call rhythm is of course well known: pulse rhythm, sun rhythm, contraction/expansion, ratios like four to one. These rhythms are relationships of two polarities that are held together by movement, activity. Such polarities do not change; their activity is mostly repetition. Rhythmical processes [by contrast] do not repeat, they have direction and are irreversible—every section is different from every other one. During potentizing, the lower, middle and upper zones have different attributes. Rhythmic processes are bound up with substance, they transform it. Substance serves rhythmic events merely as a base, a vehicle. The rhythm of one to four can be connected to a wide range of substances. Such rhythms are semi-spiritual.[56] There is also a third kind of rhythm—those that fluctuate between more and less, between a maximum and a minimum, as in a wave of water. The many so-called bio-rhythms are of this kind—the life rhythm, blood-sugar rhythm etc. There is activity and movement in all rhythms, but in different ways: in a rhythmic process the attributes of substances are altered; rhythm in the usual sense connects polarities; in its third form, rhythm increases or diminishes itself. These three kinds of rhythm are associated with the threefold human organism: rhythmic processes to the upper, head system; the increasing/decreasing rhythm to the metabolic system; usual rhythm to the middle, rhythmic system.

Potentizing, the 'step' process—in other words, the rhythmic process—takes substance through three 'zones' [or conditions], in each of which different qualities and forces in the substance come to light. Any natural substance can be potentized. Significantly, this means that the three conditions are general principles that can be drawn out of all substances. They are united in some way in every substance. (Whether purely synthetic substances can also be potentized remains to be seen from experimental research.)

Hitherto the three attributes and force-zones have only been described vaguely as ponderable, imponderable and middle conditions. Can we characterize them more precisely? Here too, Steiner's indications are helpful. He urges us to take note of how a substance stands within the whole cosmic process, how it is related to the entirety of cosmic relationships.

When a substance is examined in the usual way today in a laboratory, this is not taken into account. The well-known chemical and physical findings, the properties of the substance, are obtained. If we take cognisance of the cosmic relationship, other qualities become apparent which elude us if our substance investigation is purely analytical. What is meant here becomes evident if we look at a plant, for example Arnica. We can analyse the plant in a laboratory and find its constituents. But we can also observe it in nature. We then realize that it is situated in the context of a great polarity which is evident in its appearance and shape and in its behaviour. With its roots it is bound to the earth, with its shoots and leaves, and above all with its flowers and seeds, it is turned towards the periphery, to the atmosphere and the forces originating from cosmic realms. It is situated within the polarity of earth and cosmos, of terrestrial and extraterrestrial influences. With its roots it is connected with forces that tend towards a central point, and in its growth, and particularly in flower and seed-formation, it shows how it also follows other forces—forces that overcome the centric tendencies and strive towards the periphery.

These peripheral forces are most clearly evident in light; the centric forces, in gravity. And we can talk of a contrasting polarity of gravity and light that permeates the whole of nature. It is the contrast of the ponderable and the imponderable. And this is where the plant is placed. With its roots it partakes in gravity, the centric element; with its flowers it absorbs imponderable energies. The centric forces are the entities researched by physics and chemistry, referred to above as central forces. The peripheral, imponderable forces remain unnoticed and uninvestigated by laboratory science. They are the universal or etheric forces. Their nature and quality were thoroughly investigated and presented by Steiner. In the half century since then, a wealth of experimental evidence and practical experience of these imponderable forces has been gathered in the most varied areas of anthroposophical work, so that today they represent a confirmed scientific fact.[57]

The plant is situated in this polarity of ponderable and

imponderable forces, giving rise in it to three 'regions': the root region, the flower/seed region, and between these two and balancing them out, the leaf region. The two realms of polar forces—the centric and peripheral—and one that holds the balance between them, permeate all of non-human nature, including the inorganic mineral kingdom, as three formative impulses, as three modes of working. The relationships we need to be aware of here are not ones we are used to. Just as there is a region in the plant where it is oriented towards lightless gravity (the root), and one where it absorbs and assimilates imponderables (the flower), and one that mediates between these two (the leaf region), so there are also three kinds of mineral activity: the realm of forces in salt formation, the realm of assimilating imponderables in the phosphorus-sulphur process, and a balancing-out region in the mercury process. In former times when people did not yet have our methods and concepts of chemical and physical investigation, and therefore looked at substances primarily from the standpoint of their context within nature as a whole, these three principles in nature were termed salt, mercury and sulphur. Salt referred to the process of dissolving, how all salt-like substances can dissolve or precipitate out of solution, how it gives itself up through gravity to the surroundings, and is free from imponderables. With sulphur we have the opposite situation. For 'the substances that are polar opposites of salt are those that absorb the imponderable—namely light, but also other imponderables, warmth and such like—and make them their own'. 'And ancient atavistic knowledge was not entirely unjustified [...] in calling phosphorus the light-bearer, because it saw very correctly that phosphorus bore the imponderable, the light. Whatever repels salt bears phosphorus within it.'[58] Between the action of salt and the action of phosphorus-sulphur is the action of mercury.

> Just as man is a threefold being—[consisting of] nerve-sense system, circulatory system, and metabolic system—and just as the circula-

Diagram 22: The three formative impulses in the plant

tory system has a mediating position between metabolic and nerve-sense functions, so in outer nature a mediating role is played by everything that neither predominantly surrenders itself like the salt element, nor predominantly assimilates imponderables, but holds the balance between these two activities by expressing itself in form of the droplet. For the mercury element is basically always that which, through its inner configuration of forces, tends towards drop form.[59]

If we take the terminology for the three types derived from the mineral element, we can apply them to the three formative impulses in the plant: the rooting process as salt; flowers, seeds, everything that tends towards assimilation of imponderables, as sulphur. The leaf region is mercurial, performing a mediating function between the flower and fruiting element that strives upwards, and the downward root element, as though seeking the balance between gravity and light. This gives us an outline of the three principles that permeate the whole of nature.

So what does all this have to do with potentizing?

What we differentiate conceptually is, in the substances of nature, always bound together. In every substance the three principles—salt, mercury and sulphur—are interwoven. *And potentizing is an unravelling of these three natural principles*. When a substance is potentized we get a separation of the three spheres of activity, whereby lower potencies draw out the salt principle, middle potencies draw out the mercury principle, and high potencies the sulphur principle. From this it is possible to say what is in the various potencies of a remedy: salty gold in Aurum D6, mercurial gold in Aurum D15, and phosphoric-sulphur gold in D30. This likewise clarifies what was referred to as 'information' above. The medium is not a carrier of information but carries the substance in its imponderable, sulphurous condition.

But what do we gain by separating the three principles and using them individually?

The answer leads to the very heart of healing. To begin with, we need to bear in mind that man is a threefold being of body, soul and spirit. The body itself is also threefold. Rudolf Steiner first presented this threefold picture of the body in his book, *Riddles of the Soul*, published in 1917, and often referred to it subsequently. The human body is arranged according to three principles: the nerve-sense system, the metabolic-limb system, and between them the rhythmic heart-lung system. These are not regions distinguished purely anatomically, but three different fields of force and function which relate to each other in the way that salt, mercury and sulphur do in nature. Indeed there is a connection whereby 'the threefoldness in the three principles of nature in the world outside man corresponds to the threefold human being'.

What does this mean for the human being, and above all for healing?

The insights required here are very alien to modern people, and can even seem highly improbable. This was not the case for Hahnemann. From his exact and dedicated observation of disease and the healing process, he was intimately acquainted with the healing properties of different substances. And he came to realize that these healing forces are not the usual qualities identified by physical-chemical means. Today a therapeutic effect is pictured as a purely chemical-physical process—a chemically defined medicine reacts with the chemically-physically reacting organism. Hahnemann did not think like this. He made a distinction between the material body and the force that gives it life:

> §9: In a healthy person the spirit-like vivifying life-force (autocracy), as a dynamic entity, holds unrestricted sway over the material body (organism), and holds all its parts in a wonderfully harmonious living process in feelings and actions, so that our indwelling rational mind can freely use this lively, healthy instrument for the higher purposes of our existence.

> §10: The material organism pictured without its life-force is incapable [by itself] of any sensation, activity, or self-maintenance[60]; only the immaterial principle (the life-principle, the life-force), that imbues the material organism with life in both health and sickness gives it sensation and activates its life-functions.[61]

This immaterial dynamic life-force, which is disrupted in illness, can only be acted upon by a correspondingly dynamized remedial power. This was Hahnemann's conviction. In his note to § 11 he writes:

> The substances in nature which we find to be remedies are only remedies in as much as they possess power (each one its own specific power) to change the human state of health through dynamic, spirit-like effects (by means of living, sensitive fibres) on the spirit-like life-organizing life-principle. [...]
>
> This effect of the remedy on our state of health occurs *dynamically* [i.e. in the realm of forces or energies], like an infection, without the material parts of the remedy being involved at all.
>
> The smallest dose of a remedy dynamized in the best way—in which by calculation there can be so little of the material left that its minuteness can no longer be thought or conceived of by the best arithmetical heads—shows *far more* healing power in the relevant case of illness than larger doses of the same remedy in substance. Each most subtle dose can therefore contain almost only the pure,

> freely released, spirit-like remedial power, and bring about such great effects *dynamically* [energetically] as could never be achieved from the substance taken in its raw form even in larger doses.

From his fine observation and experience Hahnemann discovered that there are forces other than chemical ones in substances, and that these others are the real healing forces which must first be drawn out by potentization. This experience was confirmed by Rudolf Steiner's spiritual science. In the course for doctors mentioned above, Steiner raises the question:

> Does sense-perception and everything that is similar to it give us any clue about the somewhat differently constituted influences that are supposed to flow from a medicine into the human organism? As we know, we have three influences in the human organism in its normal condition. Firstly, the influence from sense-perceptions, which is transmitted through the nervous system. Secondly, we have the influence through the rhythmic system, breathing and circulation. And thirdly, the metabolism. These three normal interrelationships must have some kind of analogy in the abnormal relationship that we create between the remedy, which we must take in some form from external nature, and the human organism.[62]

He then discusses, citing many facts, 'that there is an inner relation between the human being and the non-human world'. From this we are challenged to become clear 'on what basis the healing relationship of the human being to non-human nature exists at all'.[63]

He then states an almost startling piece of knowledge:

> The organism is confronted, in what is in bodies of the outer world, with something with which it has no healing relationship, that it therefore receives [in medical treatment] as a foreign body. As a result, a terrible work load and disruption is imposed upon the organism when we burden it with all the forces that come into play when we administer medication in an allopathic form. We will later discuss the cases in particular where it is possible to remove this homeopathizing process from the body.[64]

Immediately prior to these sentences Steiner had described the relationship between allopathy and homoeopathy from a spiritual scientific perspective, and now makes a really surprising statement:

> From what spiritual science finds, there is basically no allopathy. In reality there is no such thing as allopathy because even what is prescribed as allopathic medicine undergoes a homoeopathizing process in the organism, and the actual healing is done through this homoeopathizing process. This means that every allopath finds support for his allopathic procedure from the homoeopathizing of the organism itself, which actually carries out what the allopath leaves undone, namely, the [cessation or] suspension of the relationship between the individual parts of the remedial substance. Certainly it makes a considerable difference whether we relieve the organism of this kind of homoeopathizing or not, for the simple reason that the healing process in the organism is indeed connected with the conditions that gradually arise when a remedy is homoeopathized.[65]

Then follows the earlier quotation saying that the organism does not have a therapeutic relationship with things as they are in the external world. And he adds:

> So you see that the homoeopathizing process is basically something that to a certain extent has been very carefully taken from nature itself, even though fanaticism has made significant steps against it as we shall still see.[66]

With this insight Rudolf Steiner clarified the significance of potentizing. It is to be found in the sphere of healing. *Potentization creates a healing relationship between the human being and external nature by taking substances found in nature and drawing out of them their actual healing power*. But substances only have a healing effect when they are in their salt, mercury or sulphur condition. So, in order to be able to treat the human being with salt-element, mercury-element or phosphorous-element, it is a matter of drawing this out, of separating it in some way from that with which it is otherwise bound up. And earlier forms of chemistry paid the greatest care and attention to this process.

Drawing out the three nature principles was a long and laborious path for the doctors and pharmacists that worked with them, which today has dried up. We must find another way.

> We can use the method that was employed when the old way had dried up, but was employed out of a still-distinct feeling that the human being is something more than just a retort. And this is the method whereby we simply try to make useful the forces that are at the foundation of the substances we find, by taking those substances and potentizing them. This essentially is the approach taken by Hahnemann and which, I would like to say, represents a new ascent by the total medical striving of humanity after the old methods had dried up, when extraterrestrial or other such connections were no longer known.[67]

By recognizing potentization as a factor of the human organism, Rudolf Steiner was able to solve another problem: the ratio in the dosage of different potencies. Prior to this there had been no insight. The threefold graph of potency effects which he predicted, is connected to the threefold human being. Lower potencies have an effect on the lower organism, the higher ones on the head system, and the middle ones on the rhythmic system. This also shows how high we can potentize and still have a beneficial effect—up to and including the potencies of the third section of the graph, which work on the nerve-sense system. Going higher than this would make no sense since, as Steiner once said to Kolisko, the human being does not have any systems higher than this. The third section of the graph goes from potencies around the 20s to the middle 30s. Stopping at D30 is a habit that has been passed down over the years. In specific cases and for specific reasons we can of course go beyond this potency. We need to note that the zero points spoken about by Steiner and evident in plant-growth experiments, are not an indication of no effect in the substance, but are turning points where the substance attributes change and make a transition from one region of the threefold human being to the next.

Aligning the potencies to the human organism gives a secure basis for medical treatment. The choice of potency in each case comes from the doctor's therapeutic intention, experience and intuition. For every doctor who uses potentized remedies, being aware that he is dealing here with the three nature principles gives him valuable strength and energy (*Belebung*) in his will to heal, and in his medical practice. With this awareness all considerations and worries about the degree of dilution fall away. So does the feeling of having to justify oneself in terms of physics. This is an area where physics has no jurisdiction.

Diagram 23 gives an overview summary of our presentation of the potentization problem, where individual details shed light and clarify each other within the context of the whole. An understanding of potentization can fundamentally expand our knowledge of man and the world if we are open to looking at new insights. In the 1920 course Steiner says:

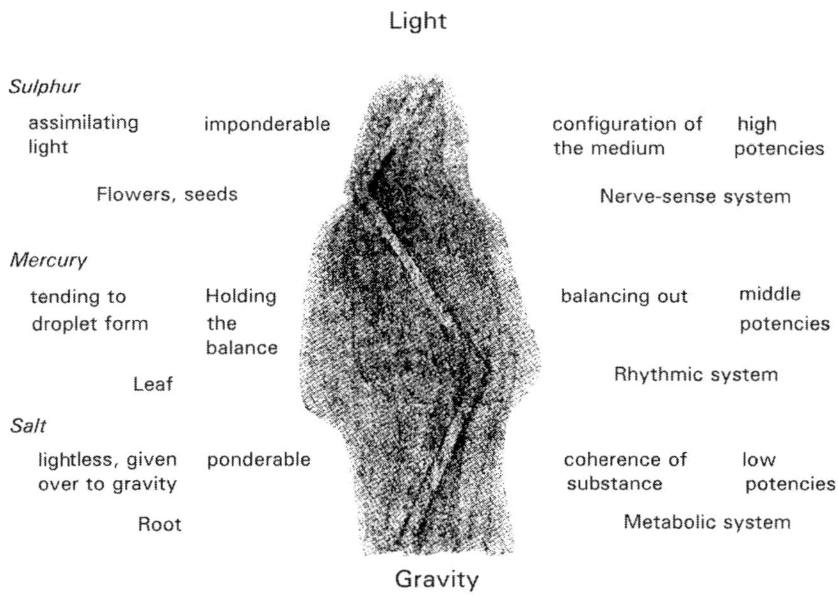

Diagram 23: The three nature principles, potencies and their relation to the threefold human being

Healthy ideas must take hold again concerning the spiritual attributes of matter. It is truly no small service that has been done in the homoeopathic tradition during the nineteenth century, that a commitment to the spirituality of external material substance has been kept alive. This is really something of the greatest importance. For, outer allopathic medicine has unfortunately turned more and more to the belief that it is dealing only with matter, with external material effects in substances outside the human being.[68]

Summary and Looking Ahead

We have described examples from the totality of etheric formative forces. Every creature, whether plant, animal or human, when it becomes an organism, takes hold of these forces and out of them forms an *etheric body*.

The etheric body is a configuration of forces which, like a blueprint, actively permeate every organism and are the bearer of the shaping process within it; form, life and specific substance come to manifestation in time.

Rudolf Steiner also uses other names for the etheric body—body of formative forces, life-body, etheric-elemental body, and time-body—depending on which aspect of the etheric body is under consideration. We can speak of a 'body of formative forces' when we have in mind its shaping aspect, the development of form. We speak of a 'life-body' when looking at the life processes, the various living organs with their centres and rhythms, and stages of development in time. And with the 'elemental-etheric body' we touch on the secrets of specific substance, focussing on the processes and transformations of substance, how substance originates and passes out of existence, the change from life to death. And anyone who is able to observe the etheric body as a 'time-body' at every moment of life, has an overview of the life tableau in its entirety, life from beginning to end; he sees past and future life—here time becomes space.

The etheric body can indeed be perceived with supersensory 'sight' at the level of Imagination but, in order to understand and differentiate it, a minimum of Inspiration is required, along with healthy thinking.

While the capacities of higher perception are still undeveloped, a scientific thinking that is in tune with reality can be nurtured by means of an artistic training. It may seem anachronistic for a budding scientist today to be required, in addition to his studies, to train in sculpture, painting, music, poetry and eurythmy. Already in his day, Steiner recommended that institutions of higher education introduce courses in sculpture, music and artistic speech for scientists, doctors, teachers and theology students; this is done today in all anthroposophical training centres. It is thanks to Dr Gisbert Husemann that such courses[69] have been developed over decades and are currently organized by him and others as 'Knowledge of the Human Being through Art', setting a trend that now extends beyond the training for anthroposophical doctors.

Science needs to lift itself up to the arts so that it can rise to a knowledge of life, of the etheric! It is not enough that good doctors have music or painting as a hobby, that biologists and chemists are good essayists or poets, or that important physicists towards the end of their life become philosophers, discovering a late love for Sophia, the goddess Natura. In an age of science it is the scientists who bear responsibility for the view of the world and the human being that is passed on to young people in schools and colleges and becomes the guideline for their actions. It is not due to nature that her 'open secrets' are hidden, but to the self-imposed restriction of science to consider only what can be measured, counted and weighed.

This book presents the lifelong research of Ernst Marti into the etheric. Natural science is knowledge of the forces of nature. Knowledge of the ethers and formative forces is the most important contribution of anthroposophy to a broadening of science. Science is thereby enabled to see into life.

It is not the task of this book to look at consciousness and self-consciousness, the soul and spiritual element in animal and man. We can nevertheless attempt a short indication of what needs to be done in the future.

At the end of his courses on the etheric, Ernst Marti used to say — and this also applies to this book — that an important aspect of the etheric was still missing, namely, the metamorphosis of etheric formative forces into soul forces.

Anyone wishing to understand the soul in its connection with the body must first become acquainted with the etheric, for:

> These forces that are active in the etheric body, function at the beginning of human earthly life—most evidently during the embryonic phase—as formative and growth forces. During the course of life a part of these forces emancipates itself from its work of giving form and growth and becomes thought forces, those very forces that in ordinary consciousness bring forth the shadowy world of thoughts. It is of the greatest importance to realize that ordinary human forces of thought are the refined forces of form and growth. In the human organism's shape and growth a spiritual[/mental] element is revealed, for this spiritual element then appears in the course of life as the mental force of thought.[70] *

---

* [Translator's note] One of the areas emphasized by Steiner in which 'it is of the greatest importance to realize that ordinary human forces of thought are the refined forces of form and growth', is education. Steiner spoke of how etheric forces work particularly strongly on the organism of the child up to the change of teeth, after which they become 'emancipated' for other tasks of a more mental or intellectual nature. The importance of not making intellectual demands on these forces before the change of teeth is stressed again and again.

A picture which can be helpful to understand this is the following. Imagine a scenario where a group of artists of all kinds comes together and forms a co-operative for their creative activity. But first they need a suitable building. In order to make sure the building really harmonizes with their needs and the work they wish to engage in, they decide to build it themselves. They are practical people, and using a perfect architectural blueprint, they set about constructing their art centre. They work with dedication and enthusiasm, and after seven years of work they have a beautiful, strong and sturdy building. With music and movement rooms, a theatre, painting and sculpture studios, they can begin their real work, fully supported by the building. The place positively hums with creativity.

Now take a second scenario. It begins like the first with a similar group of artists. They too set about building themselves a suitable building. But now, after four years, when the building is up but not finished, some 'experts' and

Continued on next page

Thus the etheric formative forces reveal themselves on the one hand as sculpting energies in the organism, and simultaneously on the other as forces of thought in the soul. To understand their metamorphosis into the differentiated soul elements of thinking, feeling and willing, a detailed knowledge of the forces of form, life and substance must first be acquired. When this connection of the soul with the body is studied and understood, another very significant factor for all soul life becomes evident: consciousness and self-consciousness do not develop in the soil of up-building etheric functions, but on processes that are breaking down.

> [...] Spirit [or mental activity (*Geist*)] develops in the human being *not* on the basis of *up-building* functions of matter, but on *decomposing* ones. [...] The emergence of thinking in the etheric body is already founded not on a continuation of the etheric nature, but on its decomposition. *Conscious* thinking does *not* occur in processes of shaping and growth, but in those of 'unshaping', of withering and dying off, which are always part of an etheric process. In conscious

---

Footnote continued

authorities come along and complain, 'Why are you wasting your time on construction work? You are artists, you should be developing your art!' The artists feel under pressure, and reluctantly start work on their artistic disciplines while still trying to complete the building. But the building, not properly finished, doesn't support them. The roof leaks, damp rises up the walls, there are draughts, the floorboards in the movement rooms start to warp. The building is in constant need of repair and patching up. The artistic work does happen, but is often hampered by the need for repairs on the building.

These scenarios give a picture of the etheric forces working on the organism, like the artists building their art centre. When the construction is complete, the artists are now free ('emancipated') to do their artistic work, and have a strong body in which to do it.

If young children are forced into intellectual activities too early, as in the second scenario,the laying of a foundation for a healthy and strong body is weakened. Knowledge of child development from a spiritual perspective is essential for an educational system that supports and is appropriate to each stage of early development, rather than undermining it.

> thinking thoughts are released from the bodily forming processes and, as forms in the soul, become human experiences.[71]

This brings us back to our starting point where we saw the connection between sensation and formative force in nature. As in thinking, so too in perception etheric formative forces metamorphose into soul content as sense impressions, mental pictures and the formation of thoughts.

Science is now giving these facts some attention. It is at present in the process of discovering and investigating the so-called morphogenetic fields surrounding the earth. It has already observed the most astonishing phenomena of telepathy, transference of intelligence and learning, and the processing of sense impressions and memories in man and animal.* It will be able to evaluate these phenomena properly when it incorporates the ideas into its thinking that are presented here concerning the world of formative forces and their connection with sensation and the body of formative forces. Thought forces are metamorphosed formative forces, and are present as living thought structures in the sphere of the ether worlds. If sensation and other soul content such as thoughts, feelings and drives are to be found within the sphere between sky and earth, then it is not such a far step to the realization that not only are soul capacities of man and animal influenced by the atmosphere, by wind and weather, but that, vice versa, the soul content released from the body affects and changes the environment and the elemental powers.

A science that comprehends ethericity becomes a knowledge of nature that overcomes the dualism of spirit and matter. It is through the Cosmic Word, manifesting in the etheric, that everything came into being and continues to be. Ernst Marti was a master of the word and even in his 80s, in lectures and con-

---

* [Translator's note] See here particularly the work of Rupert Sheldrake, e.g. *New Science of Life; The Presence of the Past; Morphic Resonance and the Habits of Nature; Dogs that know when their owners are coming home;* to name just a few.

versations, tirelessly described to his students, medical students, colleagues and friends, how the spirit of the world creates through formative forces and elements: whoever understands the secrets of form, life and substance, also understands how the Logos speaks, sounds and contemplates through the stars.

In 1973 Ernst Marti wrote a small meditative book, *Der Prolog des Johannes-Evangeliums und die Kategorien des Aristoteles* [The prologue of St John's Gospel and the categories of Aristotle], which seems the quintessence and indeed the source of this book on the etheric.[72] He writes there:

> In St John's prologue, the 'Word', the Logos, is described as the cosmic creator in its connection with the human being [...] The prologue contains three images. It shows a threefold nature. Each image reveals a new aspect of the Logos—as star, sun, and cross. The being of Christ is revealed in these three signs. Christ is a star being, a sun being and a cruciform-spatial being. The prologue calls these

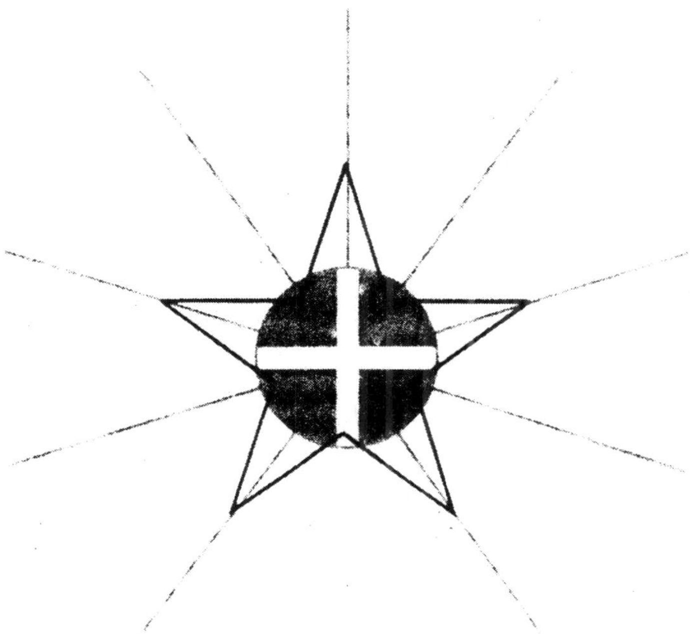

Diagram 24: The threefold being of Christ

three the Word, Life, the Light of men. They manifest as the reality of the world: a picture of the Logos appears in the starry skies; in 'in him was Life' are the sun-forces streaming through the universe; in the sun, which in its movement generates the cross of space, is 'the Light of men'.

There is another reason why knowledge of the etheric needs to spread among modern humanity. Rudolf Steiner drew attention to the fact that Christ would re-appear in the etheric during the twentieth century.[73] Jesus Christ appears, in form of the risen one, as a Living being and in a bodily substance of Light. So that humanity does not sleep through this event and allow it to pass over them unnoticed—this too is why this book was written.

May human beings take the etheric into their hearts and minds, so that it rises again and lives in their thinking!

Appendix

Irmgard Rossmann – Biographical Sketch

Irmgard Rossmann, née Brunner, was born in 1935 in Günzburg on the River Danube in Germany. She grew up with two older brothers in a family surrounded by much music and appreciation of art. She attended a humanities-oriented high school from which she graduated at 17. This was followed by half a year in England working in a home for children with special needs. She then studied medicine in Munich and Freiburg, qualifying in 1959, followed by a doctoral thesis in experimental work in a medical clinic in Munich. During her studies she was part of a student group that regularly worked on anthroposophical medical questions with Ernst Marti.

She married Dr Heinrich Rossmann in 1963 and had four children.

After a period working as an assistant doctor in Munich, Schwäbish Gmünd and Kempten, she moved with her husband in 1966 to a country practice in Kirchberg/Murr. From 1977 to 2000 she had a general practice in Munich.

After Ernst Marti's death in 1985, Irmgard Rossmann undertook the preparation and editing of his scientific estate.

She did a further training, in biography work, with Gudrun Burkhard. She gave many lectures in her own right, and also biography seminars in high schools and anthroposophical establishments.

Life and Work of Ernst Marti – An Outline

Born into an innkeeping family on 5 March 1903, Ernst Marti spent his early childhood with two younger sisters in rural surroundings in Klus by Balsthal, in the Canton of Solothurn, Switzerland. As a child he was very attached to his mother but soon became more independent and, according to a fragment of autobiography, was often out exploring nature in which he had deep experiences and early philosophical questions.

When he was eight, his family moved to Solothurn. The Martis were friendly here with the family of a Catholic priest, under whose influence Marti's cultural horizons were expanded. At the canton school at Solothurn, he learnt classical Latin, Greek and Hebrew—his original wish was to study theology—and finished there in 1923 with the highest pass mark.

He studied medicine at Genf, Zurich, Bern and Vienna. Marti became acquainted with anthroposophy and anthroposophical medicine in Vienna through an association of anthroposophical medical students. At the same time he was part of the Wandervogel movement. He qualified as a doctor in 1929 at the University of Zurich. He then worked as an assistant doctor in the Rosegg psychiatric clinic in Solothurn, and in 1931/32 in Arlesheim at the Ita Wegman Clinic (then known as the Clinical Therapeutic Institute). He also worked at 'Sonnenhof', the home for children with special needs that was attached to the clinic. He worked intensively—together with his colleagues Margarethe Kirchner-Bockholt, Madeleine van Deventer and Gerhard Suchantke—on anthroposophical medicine under Ita Wegman.

In 1931 he married Anna Gschwind whom he had known from his youth in Solothurn. In the years that followed they had a son and two daughters.

Marti began his general practice in Basel in 1932, which he would continue for around 40 years. In the following year he did his doctoral thesis, on gonorrhoeal arthritis, at Basel University.

During the Second World War, Marti saw active service as an officer in the Swiss army. After the war he organized public lectures by anthroposophical speakers such as Theodor Schwenk and Karl König—but also many others—at the Bernoullianum (in Basel University), in which Rudolf Steiner had also spoken in his day.

Marti was always ready with practical help for people in distress, particularly before and during the war and the years that followed. Jewish refugees found temporary shelter with the Martis, and after the war 'Red Cross children' were taken in by the family.

From 1948 to 1950 Marti was on the management board of the Ita Wegman Trust, and then on the initiatives committee until the end of his life. As a founding member of the Association of Anthroposophical Doctors in Germany, he was always engaged from the '50s onwards in giving lectures, particularly in the training of young medical students 'in order to awaken enthusiasm in young people and "set them on their way", and earnestly exhorting his colleagues to deepen their understanding, for example of the question of potentizing, and always to take into consideration the activity of sal, mercury and sulphur'.[1]

Marti regularly gave courses in Tübingen both for beginners and doctors. 'His particular connection with Karl König meant that many young doctors—including Gerhard Kienle—got their first experience in curative education.'[2]

Conrad Schachenmann recalled that Ernst Marti was 'a doctor through and through, and there for his patients day and night'. 'His practice was a place of help and assurance, not least because of the active background support of his wife. His unbiased observation extended to the whole person, so that the healing process was always approached in direct connection with the developments of destiny.'[3]

Marti was a very strong supporter of curative eurythmy which he practised with his patients in collaboration with his colleague of many years Margherita Ghisler, and taught in his courses for young doctors. He also worked with Rita Leroi, and later joined the doctors at the Lukasklinik in Arlesheim.

Marti wrote numerous essays and papers that were published in specialist periodicals including the *Weleda-Nachrichten*. In addition he did a great deal of lecturing both at home and abroad. In the last decade of his life he also gave courses at the pedagogical seminar at Dornach and the Akademie für Eurythmische Kunst (academy for the art of eurythmy).

In May 1984, in the midst of plans and work, Ernst Marti suffered a heart attack. This was followed soon afterwards by a stroke with loss of speech, and paralysis. In 1985, on 22 March—Goethe's death-day—Marti died at the Ita Wegman-Klinik in Arlesheim, where his work as a doctor had begun.

Notes

1. Rudolf Steiner: *Die Zwölf Sinne des Menschen* [The twelve sense of man]. In: *Menschenwerden, Weltseele und Weltengeist* [Human evolution, world soul and world spirit]. Part II: *Der Mensch als geistiges Wesen im historischen Werdegang* [Man as spiritual being in the course of history]. GA 206. Dornach 1967. Lecture on 22 July 1921, page 9–25.
2. Steiner: *Einleitungen zu Goethes Naturwissenschaftlichen Schriften* [Introduction to Goethes scientific writings], page 267–269; italicized in the original.
3. Ibid.
4. Ibid.
5. Steiner/Wegman: *Grundlegendes für eine Erweiterung der Heilkunst nach geisteswissenschaftlichen Erkenntnissen* [Foundations for a broadening of medicine according to spiritual scientific knowledge], page 27. Italics by I Rossmann.
6. Rudolf Steiner: *Der Pfingstgedanke als Empfindungsgrundlage zum Begreifen des Karma* [Whitsun as a basis in feeling for a comprehension of karma]. In: *Esoterische Betrachtungen karmischer Zusammenhänge* [Karmic Relationships]. Vol II. GA 236. Lecture of 4 June 1924. Dornach 1988, page 237–252.
7. Rudolf Steiner: *Das Geheimnis der Trinität* [The mystery of the trinity]. GA 214. Dornach 1980. Lecture of 28 July, page 30–45.
8. Johanna Zinke: *Luftlautformen* [Sounds of speech in the air]. In: *Beiträge zu einer Erweiterung der Heilkunst.* Volume 5, 1976, page 145–151.
9. Rudolf Steiner: *Eurythmie als sichtbarer Gesang ('Ton-Eurythmie-Kurs')* [Eurythmy as visible song ('Tone Eurythmy course')]. GA 278. Dornach 1984; Rudolf Steiner: *Eurythmie als sichtbare Sprache ('Laut-Eurythmie-Kurs')* [Eurythmy as visible speech ('Speech Eurythmy course')]. GA 279. Dornach 1979.
10. Steiner: *Eurythmie als sichtbare Sprache* [Eurythmy as visible speech].

11. The outermost planets discovered over the last 200 years – Uranus, Neptune and Pluto – do not, according to spiritual-scientific investigation, belong primarily to our solar system, but are 'cosmic wanderers' that have been 'caught' by the sun.
12. Further reading: Joachim Schultz: *Rhythmen der Sterne* [The rhythms of the stars]. Dornach 1963; Arnim J. Husemann: *Der musikalische Bau des Menschen* [The musical structure of man]. Stuttgart: Verlag Freies Geistesleben, 1982.
13. Frits H. Julius / Ernst-Michael Kranich: *Bäume und Planeten. Beitrag zu einer kosmologischen Botanik* [Trees and planets. Contribution to a cosmological botany]. Stuttgart: Verlag Freies Geistesleben, 1985; Ernst-Michael Kranich: *Die Formensprache der Pflanze – Grundlinien einer kosmologischen Botanik* [The language of form in plants – foundation for a cosmological botany]. Stuttgart: Verlag Freies Geistesleben, 1976. Kranich's fundamental research on the language of form in plants was extended in 1997 and reprinted under the title *Pflanze und Kosmos. Grundlinien einer kosmologischen Botanik* [Plant and Cosmos – basis of a cosmological botany] (note by F. Lohri).
14. Ernst-Michael Kranich: *Die Formensprache der Pflanze.* [The language of form in plants] Stuttgart: Verlag Freies Geistesleben, 1976, page 171.
15. Steiner: *Von der Kunst zur Wissenshact* [From Art to Science]. In: *Einleitungen zu Goethes Naturwissenschaftlichen Schriften* [Introduction to Goethe's natural scientific writings], page 134–140.
16. Rudolf Steiner: *Das Wesen des Unkrautes, der tierischen Schädlinge und der sogenannten Pflanzednkrankheiten vor dem Forum der Natur* [The nature of weeds, animal pests, and the so-called plant diseases in the forum of nature]. In: *Geisteswissenschaftliche Grundlagen zum Gedihen der Landwirtschaft* [known in English as the Agriculture Course]. GA 327. Dornach 1984. Lecture of 14 June 1924, page 149–169.
17. Maria and Matthias K. Thun: *Aussaattage* [Sowing Days]. Biedenkopf/Lahn: M. Thun Verlag, 1984.
18. Compare here the pictures in Maria Thun's *Hinweise aus der Konstellationsforschung* [Advice arising from constellation research]. Biedenkopf/Lahn: M. Thun Verlag, 1985, p 55.

19. Rudolf Steiner: *Heileurythmie* [Curative Eurythmy/Eurythmy Therapy]. GA 315. Dornach 1981.
20. Steiner/Wegman: *Grundlegendes für eine Erweiterung der Heilkunst nach geisteswissenshaftlichen Erkenntnissen*, page 28. Italics I. Rossmann.
21. Rudolf Steiner: *Kosmische und menschliche Geschichte* [Cosmic and Human History], Volume I of *Das Rätsel des Menschen. Die geistigen Hintergründe der menschlichen Geschichte* [The Riddle of Man. The spiritual background of human history]. GA 170, Dornach 1978. Lecture of 3 September 1916, pages 254–269.
22. The chart is according to Steiner from: *Kosmische und menschliche Geschichte*, page 258; the planetary signs are according to Ernst Marti.
23. Compare Rudolf Steiner: *Das Rätsel des Menschen* [The Riddle of Man]. Lecture of 13 August 1916, pages 122–142. This paragraph was taken from a lecture manuscript of Ernst Marti's with the title: *The Seven Life Processes* (note by F. Lohri).
24. From a diagram by Steiner in: *Der Mensch im Lichte von Okkultismus, Theosophie und Philosophie* [Man in the light of occultism, theosophy and philosophy]. GA 137. Dornach 1973. Lecture of 11 June 1912, pages 162–182.
25. Steiner: *Der Mensch im Lichte von Okkultismus, Theosophie und Philosophie* [Man in the light of occultism, theosophy and philosophy], page 173.
26. From a diagram by Steiner in: *Anthroposophie als Kosmosophie* [Anthroposophy as cosmosophy], part 2. GA 208. Dornach 1981. Lecture of 29 October 1921, pages 82–100.
27. Steiner: *Anthroposophie als Kosmosophie* [Anthroposophy as cosmosophy], pages 82–100.
28. Steiner: *Eine Okkulte Physiologie* [Occult physiology]. GA 128. Dornach 1978. Particularly lecture of 23 March 1911, page 68–88.
29. Ludwig Klages: *Vom Wesen des Rhythmus* [The nature of rhythm]. Kampen. Niels Kampmann Verlag, 1933.
30. Roda Wieser: *Rhythmus und Polarität in der Handscrift. Ein Beitrag zur Rhythmusforschung* [Rhythm and polarity in handwriting—a contribution to rhythm research]. Munich, Basel: Reinhardt, 1972.
31. Bernd Rosslenbroich looks at Gunther Hildebrandt's research in his book: *Die rhythmische Organisation des Menschen. Aus der*

chronobiologischen Forschung [Rhythmicity in the human organism. Results of chronobiological research]. Stuttgart: Verlag Freies Geistesleben, 1994. Ernst Marti also referred to Walther Bühler's research on cosmic rhythms (note by F. Lohri).

32. Steiner: Anthroposophical Leading Thoughts, page 221 [in German version].
33. Lili Kolisko: *Milzfunktion und Plättchenfrage* [Spleen function and the platelet question]. Dornach: Philosophisch-anthroposophischer Verlag, 1921.
34. See for example Rudolf Steiner: *Das Zusammenwirken von Ärtzen und Seelsorgern* [The collaboration of doctors and priests] in *Pastoral-Medizinischer Kurs* [Pastoral and medical course]. GA 318. Dornach 1973. Lecture of 17 September 1924, pages 134–150.
35. See Ernst Marti: *Die vier Äther* [The four ethers)]. Stuttgart: Verlag Freies Geistesleben 1981, p 16.
36. Rudolf Hauschka: *Substanzlehre* [Study of substance]. Frankfurt a. M.: Verlag Vittorio Klostermann, 1972.
37. See the chapter 'The nature of potentizing', pages 64–91.
38. Lili Kolisko: *Physiologischer und physikalischer Nachweis der Wirksamkeit kleinster Entitäten* [Physiological and physical proof of the effects of minute entities]. Published by the Arbeitsgemeinschaft anthroposophischer Ärzte. Stuttgart 1959; Wilhelm Pelikan: *Sieben Metalle* [Seven metals].
39. See Emil Pelz: *Im Dschungel der homöopatischen Potenzen* [In the jungle of homoeopatic potencies]. In *Allgemeine homöopatischen Zeitung* 216, 1971, 1, pages 25–29; Heinz Schoeler: *Das Hochpotenzproblem* [The problem of high potencies]. In *Allgemeine homöopatischen Zeitung* 216, 1971, 1, pages 17–25.
40. Steiner: *Geisteswissenschaft und Medizin* [Spiritual science and medicine].
41. Samuel Hahnemann: *Organon der Heilkunst* [Organon of the Art of Healing). From Hahnemann's handwritten revisions for the 6th edition, edited by Richard Haehl 1921. Stuttgart: Hippokratres Verlag, 8th printing 2002, page 144. ltalics in the original. The following two footnotes page 212 and 215.
42. Hahnemann: *Organon der Heilkunst* [Organon of the Art of Healing), page 176.

43. See Ernst Marti: *The Etheric, Volume I*, and *Über die vier Äther*. [On the four ethers] in *Beiträge zur Erweiterung der Heilkunst*, Issue 4, 1966. [Or see Volume I of this book.]
44. Rudolf Steiner: *Geisteswissenschaftliche Impulse zur Entwicklung der Physik* [Spiritual-scientific impulses for the development of physics]. First science course. GA 320. Dornach 2000. Lecutre of 23 December 1919, pages 25–42.
45. Kolisko: *Physiologischer und physikalischer Nachweis der Wirksamkeit kleinster Entitäten* [Physiological and physical evidence of the influence of the smallest entities].
46. Hahnemann: *Organon*, § 270, p 145.
47. Steiner: *Geisteswissenschaft und Medizin* [Spiritual science and medicine]. Lecture of 31 March 1920. Page 210–227.
48. See Georg Unger: *Die Wirkung potenzierter Heilmittel aus der Sicht des modernen Physikers* [The effect of potentized remedies from the point of view of modern physics]. In Schweizerische Apotheker-Zeitung 108, 1971, 23, pages 868–872.
49. Steiner: *Geisteswissenschaft und Medizin* [Spiritual science and medicine]. Lecture of 31 March 1920. Page 213.
50. Ibid.
51. Ibid.
52. For a description of this method see Wilhelm Pelikan: *Wirkungsnachweis potenzierter Substanzen durch Pflanzenwachstumsversuche* [Demonstration of effects of potentized substances through experiments with plant growth]. In Viktor Itschner (editor): *Potenzierte Heilmittle. Ursprung, Wesen und Wirkungsnachweis von dynamisierten Substanzen* [Potentized remedies—origin, nature, and demonstration of effects of dynamized substances]. Stuttgart: Verlag Freises Geistesleben, 1971, page 63–82.
53. See the article by Alla Selawry: *Nachweis von Gold-, Silber- und Blei-Potenzwirkungen im Kristalltest* [Demonstration of potency effects of gold, silver and lead in crystal tests]. In Viktor Itschner (editor): *Potenzierte Heilmittel. Ursprung, Wesen und Wirkungsnachweis von dynamisierten Substanzen* [Potentized remedies—origin, nature, and demonstration of effects of dynamized substances]. Stuttgart: Verlag Freises Geistesleben, 1971, page 89–101.

54. Steiner: *Geisteswissenshaft und Medizin* [Spiritual science and medicine). Lecture of 31 March 1920, page 212.
55. Steiner: *Geisteswissenshaft und Medizin* [Spiritual science and medicine]. Lecture of 22 March 1920, pages 35–53.
56. Steiner: *Anthroposophische Leitsätze* [Anthroposophical Leading Thoughts], page 221 and 223.
57. See Kolisko: *Physiologischer und physikalischer Nachweis der Wirksamkeit kleinster Entitäten* [Physiological and physical evidence of the influence of the smallest entities]; Rudolf Steiner: *Geisteswissenschaftliche Grundlagen zum Gedeihen der Landwirtschaft ('Landwirtschaftlicher Kurs')* [Spiritual scientific basis for a healthy agriculture ('Agricultural Course')]. GA 327. Dornach 1999.
58. Steiner: *Geisteswissenshaft und Medizin* [Spiritual science and medicine]. Lecture of 25 May 1920, pages 96–116.
59. Ibid.
60. Note by Hahnemann: 'It is dead and subject purely to the power of the external physical world, it decays and is resolved into its chemical constituents.' (*Organon*, page 174.)
61. Hahnemann: *Organon der Heilkunst* [Organon of the Art of Healing), page 44; the following note page 176.
62. Steiner: *Geisteswissenshaft und Medizin* [Spiritual science and medicine]. Lecture of 23 March 1920, pages 54–75.
63. Steiner: *Geisteswissenshaft und Medizin* [Spiritual science and medicine]. Lecture of 25 March 1920, pages 100, 101.
64. Ibid.
65. Ibid.
66. Ibid, page 102.
67. Steiner: *Geisteswissenshaft und Medizin* [Spiritual science and medicine]. Lecture of 26h March 1920, pages 117–137.
68. Steiner: *Geisteswissenshaft und Medizin* [Spiritual science and medicine]. Lecture of 6 April 1920, pages 312–327.
69. Arnim J Husemann (editor): *Die plastisch-musikalish-sprachliche Menschenkunde. Eine Methode des anthroposophischen Studiums* [Knowledge of man through sculpture, music and artistic speech—an anthroposophical method of study]. Special publication of *Beiträge zu einer Erweiterung der Heilkunst* [Contributions to a broadening of medicine]. Dornach 1985.

70. Steiner/Wegman: *Grundlegendes für eine Erweiterung der Heilkunst nach geisteswissenschaftlichen Erkenntnissen* [Foundations for a broadening of medicine according to spiritual scientific knowledge], page 12.
71. Ibid. page 17. Italics in the original.
72. Ernst Marti: *Der Prolog des Johannes-Evangeliums und die Kategorien des Aristoteles* [The prologue of St John's Gospel and the categories of Aristotle]. Basel: Die Pforte, 1973.
73. Rudolf Steiner: *Das Ereignis der Christus-Erscheinung in der ätherischen Welt* [The re-appearance of Christ in the etheric world]. GA 118. Dornach 1965.

Notes to 'Life and Work of Ernst Marti

1. Conrad Schachenmann, 'Ernst Marti', in Peter Selg (ed.), *Anthroposophische Ärzte. Lebens- und Arbeitsweg im 20. Jahrhundert* (Anthroposophical doctors—their life and work in the 20th century), Verlag am Goetheanum, Dornach 2000, pp. 308–10.
2. Michael Toepell, 'Ernst Marti', in Bodo von Plato (ed.), *Anthroposophie im 20 Jahrhundert. Ein Kulturimpuls in biografischen Porträts* (Anthroposophy in the 20th century—cultural impulse in biographical portraits), Verlag am Goetheanum, Dornach 2003, pp. 497–9.
3. Schachenmann, p. 308.